THE SOUND OF MUSIC COMPANION

THE SOUND
OF MUSIC
COMPANION

Laurence Maslon

A Fireside Book
Published by Simon & Schuster
New York • London • Toronto • Sydney

PAGE 1: *Maurice Zuberano's storyboard sketch for the opening of the movie.*

ABOVE: *Four great collaborators: Richard Rodgers, Oscar Hammerstein II, Howard Lindsay, and Russel "Buck" Crouse (left to right) share a laugh at the beginning of rehearsals for the stage musical. The experience would continue to be, by and large, a happy one.*

To the creative artists—writers, actors, directors, producers, and more—who have brought this story to life over the last half century.

ABOVE: *The von Trapp Family, happily arrived in America, after their first singing tour, 1939. Maria and Georg von Trapp (center) welcome Johannes, the only American-born addition to the family.*

CONTENTS

FOREWORD

My first encounter with Rodgers and Hammerstein was via my father, who was the Director of Composition at The Royal College of Music. On my tenth birthday he interrupted my endless replays of "Jailhouse Rock" and insisted that he play me something. Onto the venerable 78-rpm record player was plonked Ezio Pinza singing "Some Enchanted Evening." Then Dad played it on the piano. Before he let me back to my room, he told me a story I shall always remember. In 1949, Dad's music publisher at Chappells, Teddy Holmes, had played him "Some Enchanted Evening" and said "this will send the birth rate up." I can't remember whether I completely understood what Holmes was driving at, but on my tenth birthday Rodgers and Hammerstein joined Elvis Presley and The Everly Brothers as heroes.

Few remember in what disregard, particularly in '60s Britain, the musical was held by young people. Opinion makers held that some of the most heinous examples were Rodgers and Hammerstein's masterpieces. My own interest in their music as a young man was unusual, to say the least. Shows like *Carousel* were considered sentimental beyond the pale.

When I was thirteen, I wrote a fan letter to Richard Rodgers and, amazingly, I got a reply. As a result I was allowed to sit in on a couple of rehearsals for the London production of *The Sound of Music* and watched the show develop. Even then I wondered how casting a younger Maria, a Maria who really does climb a tree and scrape her knee, would affect the show. With a young Maria, surely the whole evening becomes a far more daring event? How would a daughter who is sixteen going on seventeen feel about her father falling in love with a girl close to her own age?

My friends at Westminster School would constantly laugh at my interest in musicals and took great delight in reading me the reviews for *The Sound of Music*, which appeared on May 19, 1961. "Look, *The Times* says the show is treacly," and "If you are a diabetic who craves sweet things, take along some extra insulin and you will not fail to thrill to *The Sound of Music*," they crowed. If nothing else, I had learnt my first lesson in creative theater advertising. For, "You will not fail to thrill to *The Sound of Music*" was the main quote outside London's Palace Theater for many years to come. When the sign finally came down, Rodgers and Hammerstein's last collaboration had become the longest running American musical in London theater history (a record only overtaken by *Chicago* in 2005).

Great melody has always deeply affected me, and Richard Rodgers is one of the 20th century's greatest tune writers. This is not to deny Hammerstein's enormous contribution. The simplicity of his lyrics is truly deceptive. Rodgers and Hammerstein wrote five of the most successful musicals of all time. Over forty years later the partnership has not yet been equaled. It probably never will be.

My long-held ambition to stage a revival of *The Sound of Music* has finally become a reality. My thanks are due to David Ian and Live Nation and all at the Rodgers and Hammerstein Organization for helping to realize the dream. I hope this companion book will explain to you why *The Sound of Music* means so much to me and every true fan of musical theater.

Andrew Lloyd Webber
London, September 2006

INTRODUCTION

Many of the world's great musicals aren't based on stories that automatically sound like brilliant ideas. A flower girl transformed by an emotionally distant professor into a woman acceptable to society? *Romeo and Juliet* reimagined as the story of a New York City gang war? A Welsh woman sent to a foreign country to teach the multitudinous children of the ruler? A beautiful young opera singer lured into the dark lairs beneath a haunted opera house? A would-be nun sent to be a temporary nanny to the children of an ex-Naval officer?

But it is due to the magic of musical theater that these all served as the bases for classics. And this last idea—a true story, as it happens—prompted the creation of what has become the most beloved musical of all time. This book tells how that musical came to be, how it thrives on stages and movie screens around the world, and how its legacy has continued for nearly half a century with no sign of slowing down. That musical is, of course, *The Sound of Music*.

The success of *The Sound of Music* is nothing short of extraordinary. Audiences began embracing it during its pre-Broadway engagements in New Haven and Boston in 1959. It ran on Broadway successfully and went out across the United States on many long tours. It was mounted in London, where for many years it held the record as the longest-running American musical in that city. Thus began its peregrinations around the globe, where it has appeared in productions large and small ever since. And of course, there is that movie . . . Made by 20th Century Fox in 1965, it is, by any estimation, the most successful movie musical in history.

Rodgers and Hammerstein were masters at creating musicals in which characters face their own lives and problems with honesty and clarity. The composer (Richard Rodgers) and the lyricist (Oscar Hammerstein II) were such a unified team that their work comes across almost as a single expression—try looking at the words for "Do Re Mi"

and not hearing the melody that was composed to go with them, for example. The fact that they wrote five of the world's most cherished stage musicals (*Oklahoma!*, *Carousel*, *South Pacific*, and *The King And I* in addition to *The Sound of Music*), one much loved movie (*State Fair*), and one classic original television musical (*Cinderella*) as well as four more stage musicals, and all in the space of seventeen years, is a remarkable achievement in anyone's book.

In the case of *The Sound of Music*, they had important collaborators in Howard Lindsay and Russel Crouse—playwrights, producers, and generally men of the theater, every bit as much Broadway royalty as were Rodgers and Hammerstein. Along with their star, Mary Martin, Lindsay and Crouse brought the idea of depicting the life of Maria von Trapp to Rodgers and Hammerstein, and the four men created a narrative of such collaborative acumen that people have been fascinated to discern what is fact and what is fiction ever since. (This book will help you figure that out.) The four-sided partnership worked: Lindsay and Crouse's libretto informs and illuminates the Rodgers and Hammerstein score as the score enhances and elaborates the Lindsay and Crouse libretto.

For Rodgers and Hammerstein, it seems remarkable that two men, each of whom had been working in the musical theater for well over thirty years, could create a score as youthful, and yet wise, as the one they wrote for *The Sound of Music*. Many of their biggest hit songs are from this show—"Edelweiss," "My Favorite Things," "Do Re Mi," "Climb Ev'ry Mountain," and the title song, among others. It proved to be their last collaboration, as Oscar Hammerstein II died the August following its November opening. I have always found it fitting that as the curtain falls, the word being sung is "dream," a word and a notion he believed in so passionately. Just think of the many times "dream" appears in lyrics he wrote over his long career.

ABOVE: *An extraordinary couple: Rodgers and Hammerstein at the height of their fame as songwriters, producers, publishers—men of the theater.*

Rodgers and Hammerstein live on today through the organization I am privileged to run. As successful creative artists are wont to do, Rodgers and Hammerstein made the decision to control their own fate. They knew how the world of Broadway worked, and they knew how the musical theater worked, so they centralized their business in one place. As their own producers and music publishers, they were also in a position to provide those services to others. They produced several Broadway plays and one musical for which they did not write the score: *Annie Get Your Gun*. In the 1950s, they branched out to Hollywood to produce the movie versions of *Oklahoma!* and *South Pacific*. Today, we are the central clearinghouse for all things Rodgers and Hammerstein related, and we take special pride in working not only to keep their great works alive, but in finding new ways to introduce them to successive generations of musical theater enthusiasts.

There is only one other place similar to the Rodgers and Hammerstein Organization and that is Andrew Lloyd Webber's Really Useful Group. So it is entirely fitting that, as I write this, Andrew Lloyd Webber and The Really Useful Group are producing a major new production of *The Sound of Music* for London's West End. It is similarly fitting that the Rodgers and Hammerstein Organization represents the work of Andrew Lloyd Webber for stage performances in North America.

The Sound of Music remains at the top of the list of the popular Rodgers and Hammerstein shows. Laurence Maslon, the author of this book, has done a marvelous job of digging behind the behind-the-scenes to find tidbits of information that help clarify just how good a story there was to begin with—and what an extraordinary job was done translating that story into a theatrical classic. This book is a welcome addition to the world of *The Sound of Music*.

Ted Chapin, President,
The Rodgers and Hammerstein Organization,
August 2006

LEFT: *Another extraordinary couple: Christopher Plummer and Julie Andrews realize the depth of their love for one another—but not in Salzburg. This is the Fox back lot, late spring of 1964.*

TRIPLICATE

(To be given to declarant when originally issued; to be made a part of the petition for naturalization when petition is filed; and to be retained as a part of the petition in the records of the court)

UNITED STATES OF AMERICA

DECLARATION OF INTENTION
(Invalid for all purposes seven years after the date hereof)

No. 9887

United States of America
District of Vermont $\}$ ss:

In the **U. S. District** Court
of **the United States** at **Burlington, Vermont**

MARIA AUGUSTA VonTRAPP

(1) My full, true, and correct name is _____
(Full, true name, without abbreviation, and any other name which has been used, must appear here)

(2) My present place of residence is **Stowe, Lamoille, Vermont**
(Number and street) (City or town) (County) (State)

(3) My occupation is **Singer** (4) I am **39** years old. (5) I was born on **January 26, 1905**
(Month) (Day) (Year)
in **Vienna, Austria**
(City or town) (County, district, province, or state) (Country)
(6) My personal description is as follows: Sex **female**
color **white** complexion **fair**, color of eyes **blue**, color of hair **brown**, height **5** feet **7** inches, weight **160** pounds,
visible distinctive marks **none**, race **white**, present nationality **Austrian**

(7) I am ___ married; the name of my wife or husband is **George**; we were married on **11/26/1927**
(Month) (Day) (Year)
at **Salzburg, Austria**; he or she was born at **Zara, Dalmatia, Austria**
(City or town) (State or country) (City or town) (County, district, province, or state) (Country)
on **April 4, 1880**; and entered the United States at **Niagara Falls, New York**
(Month) (Day) (Year) (City or town) (State)
on **December 30, 1942** for permanent residence in the United States, and now resides at **Stowe, Lamoille, Vermont**
(Month) (Day) (Year) (City or town) (County and State)

(8) I have **3** children; and the name, sex, date and place of birth, and present place of residence of each of said children who is living, are as follows:
Rosemarie, Female, Feb. 8, 1928; Eleonora, Female, May 14, 1931, said two born at Salzburg, Austria, Johannes, male, Jan. 17, 1939 at Philadelphia, Pa; all three now reside at Stowe, Vermont

(9) My last place of foreign residence was **Salzburg, Salzburg, Austria**
(City or town) (County, district, province, or state) (Country)
(10) I emigrated to the United States from **Salzburg, Austria**
(Country)
(11) My lawful entry for permanent residence in the United States was
at **Niagara Falls, N. Y.** under the name of **Maria Augsta VonTrapp**
(City or town) (State)
on **December 30, 1942**, on the **C. N. R. R.**
(Month) (Day) (Year) (Name of vessel or other means of conveyance)

(12) Since my lawful entry for permanent residence I have **not** been absent from the United States, for a period or periods of 6 months or longer, as follows:

DEPARTED FROM THE UNITED STATES			RETURNED TO THE UNITED STATES		
PORT	DATE (Month, day, year)	VESSEL OR OTHER MEANS OF CONVEYANCE	PORT	DATE (Month, day, year)	VESSEL OR OTHER MEANS OF CONVEYANCE

(13) I have **not** heretofore made declaration of intention: No. XXXXXXXXXXXXXXX, on XXX
(Month) (Day) (Year) (City or town)
in the XX
(County) (State) (Name of court)

(14) It is my intention in good faith to become a citizen of the United States and to reside permanently therein. (15) I will, before being admitted to citizenship, renounce absolutely and forever all allegiance and fidelity to any foreign prince, potentate, state, or sovereignty of whom or which at the time of admission to citizenship I may be a subject or citizen. (16) I am not an anarchist; nor a believer in the unlawful damage, injury, or destruction of property, or sabotage; nor a disbeliever in or opposed to organized government; nor a member of or affiliated with any organization or body of persons teaching disbelief in or opposition to organized government. (17) I certify that the photograph affixed to the duplicate and triplicate hereof is a likeness of me and was signed by me.

I do swear (affirm) that the statements I have made and the intentions I have expressed in this declaration of intention subscribed by me are true to the best of my knowledge and belief: SO HELP ME GOD.

Maria Augusta von Trapp
(Original and true signature of declarant without abbreviation, also other name if used)

Subscribed and sworn to (affirmed) before me in the form of oath shown above in the office of the
Clerk of said Court, at **Burlington, Vermont**
this **21st** day of **January**, anno Domini 19**44** I hereby certify that
Certification No. **3 242161** from the Commissioner of Immigration and Naturalization, showing the lawful entry for permanent residence of the declarant above named on the date stated in this declaration of intention, has been received by me, and that the photograph affixed to the duplicate and triplicate hereof is a likeness of the declarant.

[SEAL]

AUSTIN H. KERIN,
Clerk of the **U. S. District** Court.
By _____
Deputy Clerk.

Form N-315
U. S. DEPARTMENT OF JUSTICE
IMMIGRATION AND NATURALIZATION SERVICE
(Edition of 11-1-41)

16—19119-1 U. S. GOVERNMENT PRINTING OFFICE

CHAPTER ONE
VIENNA TO SALZBURG

Of all the many thrilling images surrounding *The Sound of Music*, it is the least glamorous —and yet, it is the one that tells the most tales.

On her Declaration of Intention to become an American citizen, Maria Augusta von Trapp reveals some brief facts that contain the most essential elements of her outsize personality: her birthplace (Vienna); the name of her husband (Georg von Trapp); her occupation (singer). Her distinctive marks are listed as "none"; then again, "sheer force of personality" would never have appeared in that category. Before her signature, in boldface letters, appear the words SO HELP ME GOD. God had helped Maria von Trapp many times—and she would continue to help Him.

But it is the photograph that is most revelatory: the thirty-nine-year-old woman stares straight ahead, framed by the fringes of her Austrian folk dress, although she had left her native country more than a half-decade earlier. Her pellucid blue eyes reveal a drive and determination to meet the challenges of her new country; grounded in the foundations of her faith and family, she seems poised to climb the mountains of her future. This is no flibbertijibbet, no will-o'-the-wisp, no clown.

When she applied for American citizenship in 1944, Maria von Trapp could not have predicted where her wanderings would take her, or how her story would be told, or that it would be told in every corner of the world. Maria von Trapp's story is one of exploration and faith, of obstacle and achievement, the kind one finds only in missionaries or musical-comedy heroines. And, typical of her wide-ranging personality, she was both.

This is the story of Maria von Trapp and the story of her story. It ends where it begins, for as T. S. Eliot once wrote: "We must not cease from exploration and the end of all our exploring will be to arrive where we began and to know the place for the first time."

There is an old showbiz adage about stage-struck infants being born in a trunk. Maria did it her own way—she was born on a train, a harbinger for her wanderings. On January 25, 1905, shortly before midnight, Maria Kutschera came into the world. Her mother wanted to spend her pregnancy in her native Tyrol, in the mountains in the west of Austria, but her husband insisted they come back to Vienna, where they lived, so their child could be born there. Precocious from the start, Maria made her debut before the train could pull into the Westbanhof station; she was delivered by the train conductor. Her mother was promptly escorted to the General Hospital so that Maria's birth certificate could read "Vienna."

This giddy story with a happy conclusion is the first of Maria's life and the last of its kind for many years. Her mother died when she was three; her father, a melancholy and self-absorbed man, left her in the care of foster parents. His occasional visits with young Maria were marred by his inability to understand, let alone care for, a little girl. Maria's father died in his book-laden apartment when she was nine. Maria was then sent to a distant relative whom she referred to as Uncle Franz. Their relationship was, if possible, even worse than the one Maria had with her father. Uncle Franz was imperious, abusive, and so discouraging to Maria's youthful exuberance during her teenage years that she willfully decided to cross him at every turn. He must not have been surprised—nor disappointed—to discover, upon waking from his nap one afternoon, that Maria had stolen all the spare change from his wallet and run away from home.

Maria found herself on a train once again, this time journeying west to a resort town in the mountains, in order to earn some pocket money. After the summer, she returned to Vienna with her own money and enrolled in the State Teachers' College of Progressive Education. Maria had a wonderful time in school, free at last to enjoy the comrade-ship of her classmates. She spent her days in a variety of outdoor activities—hiking, games, mountain climbing— and turned into a rugged, tanned tomboy. Her true passion, however, was for the religious music that spilled out of Vienna's churches at various masses and concerts. Maria was not the least bit interested in the religious content of the concerts; when it came to her Catholic faith, young Maria was almost exclusively interested in, shall we say, the sound of its music.

PAGES 16–17: The hills are alive: Salzburg's native beauty is framed by two rivaling mountains separated by the Salzach River—the "Capuchin's Mountain" or Kapuzinerberg, and the "Monk's Mountain" or Mönchsberg. In the middle of the church steeples, one can spot the red-domed Nonnberg Abbey, a key setting for The Sound of Music.

ABOVE AND RIGHT: Maria Augusta Kutschera: our heroine. In these two pictures, she displays two of her favorite hobbies: climbing mountains and the sound of music.

One day after graduation, Maria went on a hiking excursion in the Alps. She was an expert climber, so the guide allowed her to bring up the rear. Standing alone on a glacier, Maria observed the kind of sunset that God creates in his best moments. Some months earlier, a Jesuit priest had kindled in Maria a small spark of religious devotion, and that sunset fanned it into a flame. Maria Kutschera had her own epiphany. As she put it in her 1972 memoir, *Maria*:

> Suddenly, I had to spread my arms wide and shout, "Thank You, God, for this great wonderful creation of Yours. What could I give you back for it?"
> At that moment it crossed my mind that the greatest thing I could give to Him was the very thing I was so greatly enjoying. In other words, give up mountain climbing . . . give up living out in nature, and bury myself in a convent which, to my recollection, was a dark place of medieval character . . . I walked straight down the slope and said good-bye to my colleagues.

That Maria would give up, of all things, climbing mountains to begin the next great journey of her life is yet another delicious irony in her saga.

Maria boarded another train, this time going west to Salzburg. If there is any destination, other than Rome, for a spiritual conversion, it is Salzburg—called by some "The Rome of the North." Its two main Catholic institutions were founded as far back as AD 700. St. Rupert, considered the patron saint of Salzburg, formed a cathedral monastery among the ruins of some Roman buildings on the southern side of the Salzach River and named it after St. Peter; his niece, Avendrid, founded a convent high above a hill overlooking St. Peter's and called it Nonnberg Abbey.

It was Nonnberg Abbey that a local policeman recommended to the young lady with the rucksack and the milk-chocolate-brown suntan when she asked him which was the strictest convent in town. Maria marched up the 144 steps to the glorious baroque abbey, the red-onion dome of which is still one of Salzburg's architectural jewels. She called at the huge wooden front door and asked to see "the boss." Unbelievably, she was ushered straight in to see the Reverend Mother Abbess; she planted her feet and announced that she was there to stay.

Such forthright innocence must have been bewildering to the Mother Abbess. To march into one of the strictest and most respected convents in Europe and demand a spot on God's team is akin to a window washer climbing through a thirty-second-story office window and demanding to become the CEO of General Motors. One does not simply sign up to become a nun. There is a long and careful process. First, one may be accepted as a postulant for a trial period of probation and education; depending on the religious order, this may go on for weeks or months. Next, one is entered into the novitiate, a period lasting a year or more, where the candidate lives with other novices, under the watchful eye of the Mistress of Novices, to see how she fits in to the disciplined and arduous work of giving one's self to Christ. As the founder of the Benedictine Order, St. Benedictus wrote: "Let not the newly arrived candidate be admitted too easily, but let care be taken, as the Apostle St. John advises, to try the spirits if they be of God."

If any spirits were tried at Nonnberg Abbey, they were those of the Mistress of Novices. Maria, by her own admission, had little discipline growing up and she was more than a bit of a tomboy. She was bursting at the seams with the desire to gossip, or simply talk, to her fellow

LEFT: The dignity of Nonnberg Abbey has been legendary in Salzburg for more than 1,300 years; in addition to its spiritual leadership, the Abbey has also been a force in education for the children of Salzburg.

"SUDDENLY, I HAD TO SPREAD MY ARMS WIDE AND SHOUT, 'THANK YOU, GOD, FOR THIS GREAT WONDERFUL CREATION OF YOURS. WHAT COULD I GIVE YOU BACK FOR IT?' " MARIA AUGUSTA VON TRAPP

novices; she constantly broke things; and she loved to whistle and sing. These were not the characteristics of a young lady destined to become a bride of Christ. Yet, Maria had an intuitive intelligence and became an excellent teacher to the fifth-graders who were brought to Nonnberg Abbey for their lessons. Finally, after months and months at Nonnberg, it seemed that Maria had finally turned a corner and was ready to graduate from her novitiate.

And then came a summons from the Mother Abbess. Maria wondered what she had done now. The Reverend Mother asked her what was the most important thing in life and Maria responded that it was "to find out what was the will of God and then go and do it." Then the Reverend Mother explained what, in her mind, was the will of God for Maria: there was a widowed naval captain named Baron von Trapp living near Salzburg, in a small suburb called Aigen,

and he had been left with seven motherless children. One of them had contracted scarlet fever and was no longer able to walk the four miles back and forth to school each day. The little girl would require a private tutor and Maria would be loaned out from the Abbey for ten months to tutor her. A captain with seven children! It seemed the most fearsome thing in the world to Maria, but the Reverend Mother gently reminded her that it was God's will.

So it was that, in the fall of 1926, Maria Kutschera, wearing a second-hand brown dress surrendered by the most recent postulant and armed with only a guitar and a satchel full of books, left the sanctuary of the Abbey for the bus station to Aigen. She was starting yet another journey, this time into the unknown world of family and responsibility.

It would require all the confidence she could muster.

OPPOSITE: When location filming began for The Sound of Music, *the nuns at Nonnberg Abbey gave permission for exterior shooting only. Here, in front of the gates to the actual abbey, Julie Andrews as Maria embarks on her journey to the von Trapp villa. Of all the sequences in the movie, this shot may be the one that most closely approximates the historical reality.*

MARIA

She climbs a tree and scrapes her knee,
Her dress has got a tear.
She waltzes on her way to Mass
And whistles on the stair.
And underneath her wimple
She has curlers in her hair—
I've even heard her singing in the Abbey!

She's always late for chapel—
But her penitence is real.
She's always late for everything
Except for every meal.
I hate to have to say it
But I very firmly feel
Maria's not an asset to the Abbey.

I'd like to say a word in her behalf:
Maria . . . makes me . . . laugh!

How do you solve a problem like Maria?
How do you catch a cloud and pin it down?
How do you solve a problem like Maria?
A flibertijibbet!
        A will-o'-the-wisp!
            A clown!

Many a thing you know you'd like to tell her,
Many a thing she ought to understand,
But how do you make her stay
And listen to all you say?
How do you keep a wave upon the sand?
Oh, how do you solve a problem like Maria?
How do you hold a moonbeam in your hand?

When I'm with her I'm confused,
Out of focus and bemused,
And I never know exactly where I am.
Unpredictable as weather,
She's as flighty as a feather—
She's a darling!
        She's a demon!
            She's a lamb!

She'll outpester any pest,
Drive a hornet from his nest,
She could throw a whirling dervish out of whirl.
She is gentle,
She is wild,
She's a riddle,
She's a child.
She's a headache!
        She's an angel—
            She's a girl . . .

How do you solve a problem like Maria?
How do you catch a cloud and pin it down?
How do you solve a problem like Maria?
A flibertijibbet!
        A will-o'-the-wisp!
            A clown!

Many a thing you know you'd like to tell her,
Many a thing she ought to understand,
But how do you make her stay
And listen to all you say?
How do you keep a wave upon the sand?
Oh, how do you solve a problem like Maria?
How do you hold a moonbeam in your hand?

Every well-written musical sets up its leading characters quickly, efficiently, and theatrically. *The Sound of Music* is unique in that it has not one, but two, songs to set up its heroine. The song "The Sound of Music" is Maria's opening number; it tells us who she is, what makes her tick, what she yearns for. The second number, "Maria" (perhaps better known, but incorrectly so, as "How Do You Solve a Problem Like Maria?"), supplies a healthy corrective for the audience. Perhaps the Maria we saw in the opening number isn't such an admirable, carefree character after all. Perhaps she needs maturity and discipline. Perhaps she is, in fact, a problem.

The nuns' responses to her high jinks also reveal a good deal about them: one is tolerant, one is censorious, one is amused, but all are mystified. When Oscar Hammerstein read the first draft of Howard Lindsay and Russel Crouse's treatment of Maria's story, he was taken with a detail in the opening scene at the Abbey: Maria wore curlers under her wimple. He asked Lindsay and Crouse if he might steal that conceit for a lyric: "Would you kill me if I used it for a song?" asked Hammerstein. As a perfect example of their respect for their collaborators, Lindsay and Crouse graciously assented and Hammerstein used several of their ideas for this song.

In the movie version, the casting of the Mother Superior and the nuns was particularly effective in highlighting their contrasting personalities. Peggy Wood, the Mother Abbess (tolerant), had come from a successful operetta and television career. Sister Berthe (censorious) was played by Portia Nelson, a sophisticated actress, singer, and songwriter. Sister Margaretta (amused) was Anna Lee, a former British movie star and married to the director of *Mary Poppins*. Sister Sophia (undecided) was played by Marni Nixon, making her on-screen movie debut. Nixon was Hollywood's reigning queen of vocal dubbing, having sung for, among others, Audrey Hepburn as Eliza in *My Fair Lady*. Julie Andrews had originated that role, so *The Sound of Music* would be the first meeting between the Broadway Eliza and the Hollywood voice of Eliza, but Andrews and Nixon became good chums on the set.

Some critics have suggested that it is a bit unfair when "Maria" is reprised as choral counterpoint to the Wedding Processional in Act Two—why continue to criticize her behavior? But that is exactly the point—the nuns have finally discovered how to solve a problem like Maria: have her fall in love and live happily ever after.

PAGE 25: The nuns at Nonnberg are thoroughly bewildered by Maria—Boris Leven's Hollywood set captures the Gothic gravity of the situation.

PAGES 26–27: Always late for everything: among the nuns waiting for Maria are Peggy Wood as the Mother Abbess, Portia Nelson (right of Wood), Anna Lee (right of Nelson), and Marni Nixon (far right).

LEFT: Oscar Hammerstein's small fixes (in red) for "Maria"; written during the end of the Boston tryout, they were the last lyrics he wrote in his stage career.

ABOVE: Getting to be a habit with me: It must have been awfully hot on the Fox lot for these poor actresses, all clad in black in the California sun.

CHAPTER TWO
SALZBURG TO AMERICA

There was a time when warfare was practiced by gentlemen as gentlemen.

Robert Whitehead was a gifted British inventor who, in 1866, invented a way to deliver an explosive device underwater without detection: he called it a torpedo. The British naval authorities listened to Whitehead's pitch for his new device, but politely declined to take him up on his offer. A weapon the enemy could not see coming was just not sporting.

In 1856, Whitehead had moved his family to Fiume (then part of the Austro-Hungarian Empire) to take a job as manager of a metal foundry. It is here that he developed the torpedo, and subsequently became a celebrity. In 1909, Whitehead's granddaughter Agathe was playing the violin at a society ball attended by the cream of Fiume's society, which included many dashing young naval officers stationed there. She caught the immediate attention of a dark, thoughtful, twenty-nine-year-old captain, Georg Ritter von Trapp.

Von Trapp himself inherited the legacy of a fine naval tradition. His father had received the honorific "von" from Emperor Franz Joseph for valor while commanding his own ship. The navy captain, with his long gold-buttoned tunic and striped cuffs, made an impression on Agathe, and by 1911, they were married. In 1914, the von Trapps' domestic security was upended by World War I. A heroic and canny sea commander, Georg von Trapp was called immediately into the service of his country. Over the next four years, he distinguished himself as a submarine commander in the Imperial Navy and, for his conduct, was awarded both the Maria Theresa Cross and the title of Baron.

When Georg returned to his wife in 1919 after the end of the war, much had changed. For one thing, he had fought on the losing side. The victorious Allies drew up the Treaty of Versailles, which would go far to dismantle the world that Georg von Trapp knew and defended. Austria lost all of its seaports on the Adriatic, and the Imperial Navy was stripped to its roots; only a handful of battleships remained and all submarines were taken out of active service. Nothing is harder on a naval officer than to lose command of his ship, and now there were not even ships left for Georg von Trapp to command.

After the final curtain came down disappointingly on the theater of war, Baron von Trapp would have to devote himself to developments on his own personal home front.

Before the war, and during his occasional leave, Georg and Agathe had begun a family. There were eldest son Rupert (b. 1911), followed by Agathe (b. 1913), Maria (b. 1914), Werner (b. 1915), and Hedwig (b. 1917). The family had been forced to move several times during the war and, between von Trapp's lack of office and postwar economics, finances were tight. They resettled in a relative's house outside of Vienna and had two more children: Johanna (b. 1919) and Martina (b. 1922). The situation was often stressful, but the family relied on one another, on relatives, and on the structure and deference that aristocracy carries with it.

And then an epidemic of scarlet fever struck. In September 1922, only months after the birth of Martina, Agathe died and left the Baron with an even greater challenge—being the widowed father of seven young children. Thankfully, his children were by all accounts self-sufficient, optimistic, and supportive of their father and

one another. In 1925, Baron von Trapp relocated to a villa in Aigen, outside of Salzburg, with his children and a small domestic staff. A charming yellow structure with green shutters and a slight mansard roof, the villa Trapp was an elegant, but by no means palatial, estate. It was a brisk walk from the railway station at Aigen, accessible through a gate at the rear of the property. The gate ran along a large garden to the front of the house. There was a bell in the front, and it was this bell that the family retainer, Hans, answered when Maria Kutschera reported for duty in 1926.

The Baron was away on business and so Maria was introduced to her pupil by the housekeeper. It was love at first sight—and second, third, fourth, fifth, sixth, and seventh, as she met all the von Trapp children. Maria's very lack of experience served her in good stead, and she relied on keeping the children—who were far closer to her own age than their father was—busy by doing the things she loved best: hiking, bike riding, and singing. Especially singing.

"Music was always in the family," recalled her pupil, Maria, in a 1999 *Vanity Fair* interview. "My real mother was very musical. She played violin and piano and we all sang before we met Maria. We had at least a hundred songs before she came. What she did was teach us madrigals, and of course this is very hard to do, but we found it was no problem for us."

The Baron seemed pleased but kept his distance, joining them only for the occasional bicycling trek or hike through the hills. His was a sweet presence, somewhat muted by the death of his wife and the loss of his career, but he was by no means a stern martinet. There was, however, one constant reminder of his navy days: "My father did use a bosun's whistle," recounted Johannes, the youngest von Trapp child, in a 2005 documentary. "There were signals for all the different kids. It was very effective, but the kids didn't show up marching formally. They just responded to their signal." Maria gave the Baron a wide berth and was overjoyed to hear that he was planning to remarry, to a Princess Yvonne, a distant cousin of his first wife. The Baron was indeed planning to remarry, but he tacked in a different direction: before Maria's ten-month sojourn at the villa Trapp had ended, he asked her to become the mother of his children.

PAGE 30: *Captain Georg von Trapp in his navy regalia.*

LEFT: *The von Trapp estate in Aigen: not the Hollywood version, but, with 22 rooms, perfectly comfortable.*

ABOVE: *Georg and Agathe von Trapp: Her untimely death from scarlet fever in 1922 left a vacancy for a maternal figure in the family.*

"If he had only asked me to marry him I might have not said yes, because at that time I really and truly was not in love," wrote Maria in her memoirs. "I liked him but I didn't love him. However, I loved the children, and so in a way I really married the children." But first she had to resolve her temporal crisis—after all, she was pledged to be the bride of Christ. She ran back to Nonnberg for the Reverend Mother's advice. In the stage musical, the situation is depicted this way:

MOTHER ABBESS: . . . you have a great capacity for love. What you must find out is—how does God want you to spend your love?

MARIA: I've pledged my life to God's service. I've pledged my life to God.

MOTHER ABBESS: My daughter, if you love this man, it doesn't mean that you love God less. You must find out. You must go back.

Maria listened attentively and eventually returned to Nonnberg Abbey—but not as a novice. It was at the convent church at Nonnberg that, on November 26, 1927, she became the second wife of Georg von Trapp. In the course of Maria's twenty-two-year life, there were not too many people who had made her happy, but they were all in attendance that day: the nuns of the Abbey, the Baron, and most of all, the seven children, whose lives were now irrevocably intertwined with hers.

Life continued much as before at the villa, but now the von Trapp family activities included more sophisticated musicales. The Baron often accompanied his family on violin, the eldest children learned the accordion, and Agathe picked up the guitar; the musical selection included some of the basic chamber music by Haydn, Corelli, and Handel. There was a slight diminution in the outdoor activity, however, as Maria became pregnant with two additions to the clan: Rosmarie in 1929, followed by Eleonore in 1931. The challenge of managing nearly a dozen children was met with energy and equanimity by Maria, now fully embraced

as Mother by all of them. However, the worldwide economic depression of the early 1930s reached into the green hills of Aigen as well—the von Trapp family fortune, largely the result of Agathe's family, had kept them going since the end of World War I, but it vanished nearly overnight. The von Trapps, like so many other families, large or small, noble or common, simply had to make do with less.

Maria proved to be an expert in tightening the family purse strings. She let out extra rooms in the villa in exchange for rent from boarders and turned one of the rooms into a chapel. In 1935, the local bishopric sent a young priest named Father Franz Wasner to conduct Easter Mass at the villa. When he heard the family sing their prayers in four-part harmony, Wasner, an accomplished musician himself, knew he was in the midst of something remarkable. He thought the family had the makings of a first-rate choir and, out of the sheer joy of it, began teaching the family more complicated arrangements and material suitable for an a cappella choir. About a year later, the von Trapp family choir caught the attention of Lotte Lehmann, the favorite muse of composer Richard Strauss and Vienna's premier operatic soprano. She thought the family singers had "gold in their throats" and set about convincing Georg to let his family sing in public.

When contemplating the von Trapp story, it is important to remember that the Baron came from Austrian aristocracy and that there are certain things that the upper classes—no matter how impoverished they are in actuality—simply do not do. Performing on stage would be undignified. But Lehmann was a persuasive force. That summer she was to sing Wagner at Salzburg's acclaimed music festival, and she insisted that the von Trapp family sing in one of the festival's small complementary competitions. Georg acquiesced—"for this one time."

The Salzburg Music Festival had grown from its 1920 inception into one of the foremost concert venues in Europe, with a variety of operas, concerts, and competitions performed every summer by the finest names in classical

RIGHT: Maria's wedding day: Maria von Trapp at Nonnberg Abbey, November 26, 1927.

LEFT: The von Trapp children, about a year before Maria Kutschera arrived at the ville.

From left to right:

Martina (b 1922, d. 1951) Retired from the Trapp Family Singers to get married and raise a family; she died in childbirth while the family was on tour in California.

Johanna (b. 1919, d. 1994) Joined her mother and sister to do missionary work in New Guinea, and eventually returned to Austria, where she married and raised seven children.

Hedwig (b. 1917, d. 1972) Became a teacher and moved in 1960 to Honolulu to work for a Catholic youth organization before moving back to Austria.

Werner (b. 1915) Like his elder brother, he served as a ski trooper during World War II. He became a dairy farmer in Vermont, had six children, and retired in 1979. His daughter Elisabeth is an accomplished songwriter and singer who has played Maria in a local Vermont production of the show.

Maria (b. 1914) The 'younger" Maria was Maria Kutschera's first pupil; she eventually became a missionary in Papua, New Guinea, along with her stepmother. She retired to live in Vermont.

Agathe (b 1913) Became a kindergarten teacher in Maryland, until she retired in 1993. The family's resident painter and genealogist.

Rupert (b.1911, d. 1992) Rupert was trained as a physician and was the first to leave the singing group. He served as a ski trooper in Vermont's 10th Mountain Division during World War II and eventually set up a private practice in New England.

ABOVE: An even dozen: After Maria married Baron von Trapp, they had three children of their own: Eleonore (b. 1931), also known as "Lorli" (upper left); Johannes (b. 1939), (on his mother's knee); and Rosmarie (b. 1929), (left of Johannes).

All three children followed in their siblings' musical footsteps and all settled in Vermont, where Johannes runs the Trapp Family Lodge.

music. For their stage debut, the Trapp Chamber Choir, as they were initially known, won a prize at the festival; this was no small achievement. Soon, their popularity spread and they received invitations from all over Austria and then, after performing in the main venue at the 1937 Salzburg Festival, from all over Europe. By the fall of 1937, the Trapp Chamber Choir was even engaged by a professional manager for an official European concert tour. Poor Georg von Trapp could do nothing but submit to the inevitable, and soon became the Choir's first roadie, helping his wife and children to stage manage the tour, keep the scrapbooks, and keep the faith.

What allowed the Trapp Chamber Choir to transcend being a mere novelty act was the musical genius of Father Wasner. One thinks of him as a master chef with an abundance of ingredients at his disposal: the variety of voices, the possibilities of instrumentation, and the genuine conviction that his performers had in their material. The group also hit upon an immensely satisfying mode of presentation. In the first half of their concerts, they would sing some of the great classical pieces of devotional music by composers such as Mozart, Lassus, and Palestrina; then, during the intermission, they would change into their native Austrian garb and sing a variety of local and international folk songs. The combination of sophistication and simplicity proved to be irresistible. The von Trapps also provided something else that few other groups could: a love for one another, a love for their customs, and a love for their land. The last of these affections would be sorely tested by events in the months ahead.

It is somewhat challenging, at the remove of seven decades, to portray the complicated tensions between Germany and Austria during the 1930s. George Bernard Shaw once said that England and America are two countries separated by a common language; in a more profound way, the same was true of Germany and Austria. By the end of World War I, this was a moot point: the Allies had decided that the two German-speaking neighbors and wartime allies would be officially separated and Austria would be constituted as its own Republic. But drawing up treaties and redrawing maps can do only so much to separate cultures. The idea of a coming-together—*Anschluss*—of the two German-speaking nations was always a tantalizing one, for both Berlin and Vienna. In the words of one British historian, Gordon Brooke-Shepherd, "[*Anschluss*] became a

doubly respectable idea precisely because the war victors had forbidden it."

The dream—or nightmare—of a pan-German state was resurrected by Adolf Hitler during his rise to power as chancellor of Germany in 1933. Hitler was born in Austria, and his early years there were nothing but a series of humiliations and rejections. Still, after he had moved to Germany and begun his tyrannical ascension there, he always entertained dreams of bringing the two countries together. After becoming *führer* of the Third Reich in 1934, he was more vocal about his plans, proclaiming that Austria, because of its racial commonality with Germany, should be part of the Reich. In Vienna, they were not so sure. Some Austrians were chauvinistically pro-Austria—they despised Hitler as both a Nazi and a German; some thought there could be an accommodation that would create a powerful state where Vienna would share joint rule with Berlin; and, as Hitler's Nazi Party began to grow in Austria itself, there were those who felt inspired by the new German politics as well as by German culture. But whether the Austrians liked it or not—and most of them did not—they had to deal with Hitler. Hitler's dream of *Anschluss* was only the first of his many international campaigns of deceit, blackmail, and aggression, and Austrians were unprepared for how far he would go to achieve his dream. Austria would be the first country to experience the Nazi formula for world domination.

In the late 1930s, Austrian Chancellor Kurt Schuschnigg tried a tortuous path of negotiations with Hitler in an attempt to maintain Austrian independence from the encroachment of the Reich. This proved increasingly difficult, as Nazi Party membership kept growing in the western part of Austria and, indeed, within Schuschnigg's own cabinet. On March 9, 1938, in a quixotic attempt to galvanize his countrymen, Schuschnigg decided to hold a national referendum on Austrian independence within the week. Initial support for the idea seemed promising to Austrian patriots and, for a few hours, Schuschnigg was a national hero. But all he did was to force Hitler's hand.

Hitler announced that Germany would refuse to recognize such a vote and, under threat of invasion, he demanded that the referendum be canceled. Several days of fervent negotiations, threats, and betrayals followed. On March 11, the Germans closed the border at Salzburg and

withdrew all customs officials; all traffic between the two countries stopped and troops were massing on the German side of the border. Faced with international indifference to his plight, Schuschnigg capitulated in a radio address later that evening, proclaiming that Austria would yield to the force of the Nazis so that "no German blood should be spilled." At dawn the next day, the Wehrmacht, spearheaded by the 27th Infantry Division, walked across the Austrian border without a single shot of resistance. On that March afternoon, Hitler himself crossed the border at his birthplace of Braunau am Inn, and, two days later, received a hero's welcome in Vienna, where he proclaimed "the conclusion of the greatest aim in my life: the entry of my homeland into the German Reich." A referendum was eventually held, nearly a month after the original one was scheduled, and the *Anschluss* was ratified by 99.73 percent of the voters. Soon after, the round-ups, the arrests, and the executions began.

One ironic footnote: when Chancellor Schuschnigg made his radio broadcast to the nation, to inform them of the fall of Austria, a member of his staff hobbled into the room. Crippled in both legs, he was a firm Austrian patriot, and in the silence that followed the Chancellor's radio address, he threw down his crutches, grabbed the microphone, and shouted, "Long live Austria! Today I am ashamed to be a German!" The man's name was Hammerstein.

For the von Trapp family, the Nazi invasion was an occasion for bewilderment, frustration, and anger. Like every other city in Austria, Salzburg welcomed its conquerors joyfully and signs of the occupation were everywhere, except at the villa. When asked to welcome Hitler by hanging the Nazi flag in front of his home, Georg refused; and when Hans, the family

ABOVE: *Hitler greeted with a hero's welcome in Vienna, March 14, 1938.*

RIGHT: *Celebrating on the streets of Salzburg the day the Nazis marched in: "Georg," says Max Detweiler in the stage version of The Sound of Music, "you know I have no political convictions. Can I help it if other people have?"*

THE SALZBURG TRAPP CHOIR

Management CHARLES L. WAGNER, INC.
511 FIFTH AVENUE   NEW YORK, N. Y.

retainer, admitted his own membership in the Nazi party, the von Trapps knew that the black spider of the swastika would soon engulf them in its web. The incursions into their daily lives, at first nettlesome, soon became intolerable. It began when Georg was offered the command of a submarine in the German navy. Although it was an attractive offer to be in command of a modern submarine, he declined the honor. Then, the von Trapps were asked to sing at a birthday party for Hitler. Again, they politely declined. And, finally, Rupert, the eldest von Trapp son, who had ambitions for a medical career, was offered a post in one of the better Viennese hospitals. This again seemed attractive, until Rupert concluded that the post was available because so many Jewish doctors had been removed from positions of authority in the hospital. There was, indeed, no way to stop it. The von Trapps had to leave their beloved Austria— or what was left of it. "Exile and persecution would be preferable," declared Maria in her memoirs.

Four months after the Nazi invasion, the von Trapps worked in earnest to make their discreet plans to emigrate. Georg put the question to each of the nine children: you can have your home and your friends and stay, or you can have your faith and your honor and leave—which do you choose? Of course, they were all in agreement to leave. Although leaving Austria permanently would be difficult, the von Trapps were blessed, for they had one thing that most refugees can only dream about: a job, or at least a contract. A year earlier, an American impresario named Charles L. Wagner had offered the choir a chance to sing in New York. This offer would now give them a sanctuary in the new world. Their beloved Father Wasner got permission from his superiors to join them. In August 1938, each family member packed one rucksack, pretending that they were going on a family vacation to Italy. Among the contents of the dozen rucksacks were petticoats, ski boots, a teddy bear named Timmy, and the scrapbook of the Trapp Chamber Choir's achievements. It was not the most organized way to begin a new life, but they trusted that God would provide.

Indeed, if God had ever provided the right passport, it was now. Georg von Trapp had been born in Trieste, which was once a part of the Austro-Hungarian Empire but since the end of the war was part of Italy, so his passport allowed him and his family to travel freely across the border. The family and Father Wasner calmly boarded a train, which took them into the south Tyrol, part of Italy. The next day, the border was closed. Their timing, as befits a close-harmony group, was again impeccable.

The family stayed in the small town of St. Georgen, waiting to confirm their travel arrangements to America. It was here that Maria and Georg were informed that a tenth von Trapp was on the way; on top of all their troubles, Maria was pregnant. Eventually, Wagner wired them their money and, on October 7, 1938, they traveled to London to board the SS *American Farmer*, sailing to New York. All eleven—now nearly twelve of them—had made it. The von Trapp family motto was never more appropriate or inspirational: *nec aspera terrent* or "let not adversity terrify you." It is a creed that, a decade later, would be memorably lyricized by Oscar Hammerstein in his own way for *The King and I*:

> Whenever I feel afraid
> I hold my head erect
> And whistle a happy tune,
> So no one will suspect
> I'm afraid.

LEFT: One of the von Trapp Family's first posters advertising their musical talents—and one of the last before their escape from Austria.

CLIMB EV'RY MOUNTAIN

Climb ev'ry mountain,
Search high and low,
Follow every byway,
Every path you know.

Climb ev'ry mountain,
Ford every stream,
Follow every rainbow
Till you find your dream.

A dream that will need all the love you can give
Every day of your life for as long as you live.

Climb ev'ry mountain,
Ford every stream,
Follow every rainbow
Till you find your dream.

PAGE 45: *Patricia Neway as the Mother Abbess and Mary Martin as Maria in the original cast of* The Sound of Music, *photographed for* Life *magazine by Philippe Halsman.*

ABOVE: *Julie Andrews and Peggy Wood in the same moment from the film.*

RIGHT: *Oscar Hammerstein's first draft of lyrics eventually moved to Act Two; his thoughts about "facing life."*

When Oscar Hammerstein first grappled with this number, he knew it had to express the critical moment when Maria had to face life—in fact, that was its original title: "Face Life." It would make a superb musical number on which to end Act One and provided an opportunity for a musical confrontation between the Mother Abbess and Maria. In addition, the song had the potential to be the kind of inspirational anthem that Rodgers and Hammerstein wrote so well ("You'll Never Walk Alone").

Initially, Hammerstein was most intrigued by the concept of sacrifice, and in the notion that even though a young woman has given herself to God, the greater sacrifice might, ironically, be for her to return to the world. An early quatrain ran:

> A song is no song till you sing it,
> A bell is no bell till you ring it,
> And love in your heart wasn't put there to stay—
> Love isn't love till you give it away.

Hammerstein removed that lyric, flipped the first two lines, and inserted it later in the show, during a reprise of "Sixteen Going On Seventeen" (although it was cut for the movie). The song evolved into Maria's quest to find a spiritual compass for her life. In an early draft of "Face Life," one can see Hammerstein working through the metaphors for her struggle: "Ford every stream/climb every hill." This itself was an elaboration of a lyric in "There's a Hill Beyond a Hill," a song Hammerstein had written with Jerome Kern in 1933 for *Music in the Air*: "To climb the highest mountain/To ford the deepest river/Will make you feel the zest of life."

Although the initial idea for "Face Life" began with Maria singing the number herself, it evolved to become a duet between her and the Mother Abbess, and then, in the end simply a solo for the Mother Abbess. When the final lyric was crafted as "Climb Ev'ry Mountain," Rodgers bypassed the traditional verse intro and set the lyrics with strength and fervor. Rodgers and Hammerstein knew early on that, whatever inspirational power the song might have at

ABOVE: *The finale from the Broadway stage production, 1959. In this version, Mary Martin leads the von Trapp family to safety.*

RIGHT: *The other side of the mountain: in reality, the von Trapps would have marched straight into Berchtesgaden, Hitler's mountain retreat*

PAGE 50–51: *The movie finale: Here, it is Baron von Trapp who leads the way to freedom.*

the end of Act One, it would only grow when reprised at the show's finale.

When Ernest Lehman set up the structure for the movie version, he independently went back to Lindsay and Crouse's original impulse to end the first part of the story at Maria's silent farewell to the von Trapp family, one scene earlier than "Climb Ev'ry Mountain." When the movie was first shown in theaters in 1965, there was an intermission and, as a result, "Climb Ev'ry Mountain" became the first major song of the film's "second act." Director Robert Wise felt he had to restage the song to take advantage of the increased intimacy of a movie performance, as opposed to the expansiveness of a theatrical production. "We had to find some way to do it that wasn't quite so obvious. So we got the idea of shooting it up against the wall [of the Mother Abbess' office]," he recalled on the audio commentary for a home version of the movie. It is unusual for a major number to begin with the singer's back to the camera, but that is exactly how Wise filmed Peggy Wood as she began "Climb Ev'ry Mountain." (Or, more accurately, as Margery MacKay began the song; although Wood had been an accomplished operetta star early in her career, her singing was dubbed for the movie.) "We just shot her singing and she walked over to the window," recounted Wise. "We pan with her to this window and she finishes it over there, and I think it worked very well." In addition to the simplicity of the camera movement, the chiaroscuro lighting—worthy of a Rembrandt—makes the scene both intimate and touching.

When the reprise of "Climb Ev'ry Mountain" makes its inevitable appearance in the finale, Hammerstein's words take on a literal, as well as a figurative, meaning—the von Trapps must indeed journey over mountains and rivers in order to find their freedom. The actual von Trapp family has always been bemused that the show's creators took them over the Alps to Switzerland for the final escape: "Don't they know geography in Hollywood? Salzburg does not border on Switzerland!" complained Maria von Trapp to a reporter in 1967, although the dramatic license in topography existed in the original Broadway show.

When shooting the movie, the crew compounded the problem further. Looking for the proper location for their final shot of Christopher Plummer leading the children and Julie Andrews to sanctuary, they found a mountain called Obersalzberg in Bavaria, Germany. It certainly looked the part. But back in the 1930s, on the other side of that mountain was Hitler's mountain retreat, in Berchtesgaden. So, if strict geography were being followed in the film, Baron von Trapp was leading his family straight into the headquarters of the Nazi high command—"not exactly where we wanted to be," quipped Johannes von Trapp, drily.

CHAPTER THREE

AMERICA TO BROADWAY

When the von Trapps disembarked from the SS *American Farmer* in the fall of 1938, they dragged their paltry few pieces of luggage to the Wellington Hotel on West 55th Street. Ten blocks south, at the Imperial Theater, a steamer trunk was all the rage on Broadway.

Well, not the steamer trunk exactly. The sensation was the pert, gamine ingénue sitting on top of the steamer trunk, wearing nothing but high-heeled shoes and a wolf-fur parka, seductively trimmed mid-thigh to reveal her shapely legs. The scene was set in a railroad station in Siberia; a stopgap in the story while the stagehands changed the scenery behind a curtain. These were the merry years of the musical comedy, when shows were silly and undemanding, filled with beautiful girls and beguiling songs. If the songs were entertaining enough, audiences might not mind being distracted from the story; if the songs were *really* entertaining, they wouldn't mind the story. Thank goodness the song this ingénue was singing was written by Cole Porter.

And what a song it was. The soubrette disarmingly recounts how she entertains a bevy of young men, "but my heart belongs to Daddy / 'Cause my Daddy he treats me so well." It made an overnight star out of Mary Martin, who was perched so fetchingly atop the steamer trunk. *Leave It to Me!*, a mildly satirical confection about an American ambassador in the Soviet Union, was Martin's Broadway debut. Born in Weatherford, Texas, Martin had tried Hollywood and the nightclub route with mild success before landing the inconsequential part of the ingénue in *Leave It to Me!* She was cheerful and perky, and projected an appealing innocence. Perhaps too innocent; the story goes that Martin's co-star, the buxom and bawdy Sophie Tucker, had to explain the song's manifold double entendres to her. Martin's uncloying innocence would come in handy two decades later when she would cross paths with Maria von Trapp.

While Martin was enjoying life as the toast of the Great White Way, the von Trapps were struggling with only four dollars to their name and an even more meager command of the English language. Ensconced in the Wellington, while their concert manager put their tour together, the family resisted the temptation to visit the sites, skyscrapers, and sensations of New York City. When the family immigrated to America, Maria fulfilled her natural function as head of the performing family. She would set the priorities, manage the finances, and determine the artistic direction of the Trapp Family Choir, as they were now known professionally. In many ways, the fictional roles of Maria and Georg were reversed when they came to America. Maria was the stern martinet of the troupe, dictating economy, discipline, and focus during the arduous days and nights of touring; Georg—whose performing role was largely limited to being introduced to the audience before the finale—attended to domestic details and family rituals and provided moral support.

The first national tour of the Trapp Family Choir was yet another series of wanderings across a large and frequently bewildering country. The tour started in Pennsylvania, and traveled west as far as Oklahoma before finally concluding at New York's Town Hall—one of the city's first-rank venues for classical performers—two weeks before Christmastime. With their Town Hall appearance, the von Trapps made their debut in New York's Theater District nearly twenty years to the day before the musical based on their lives would open on Broadway. The family rested briefly with friends living outside of Philadelphia, Pennsylvania, where Johannes—the only von Trapp born in America—made his debut in January 1939.

Soon the von Trapps' visitors' visas expired, and it was time for them to leave America. Returning to Austria, let alone to their villa, was an impossibility, so a brief but successful Scandinavian tour was organized. During that tour, World War II broke out, but they were lucky to get on a ship and secure passage back to America in October of 1939. Surrounded by refugees in far worse straits than they,

the von Trapps were profoundly grateful to return to New York; unfortunately, they were detained at Ellis Island for three days, after Maria made an injudicious remark about wanting to stay in America forever. Finally sprung from their detention thanks to the intervention of a Catholic charity, they were on their way to tackle another series of concert tours.

Although the nationwide concert tours were successful with audiences and critics, Maria had a suspicion that they might do better, and she contacted the manager of Columbia Concerts, Inc., one of the most formidable booking agencies in the country (they are even more formidable now as Columbia Artists Management). Their manager at CCI, Freddy Schang, had his own suspicions—that the von Trapps might be more commercially successful if they could meet their American audiences halfway by adding more English-language folksongs to their repertoire, sprucing up their costumes and makeup, and behaving less formally and more spontaneously with audiences. Normally, Maria would have planted her feet and refused to change her routine, but wisely, she listened instead and sealed the deal with Schang. He redubbed them the Trapp Family Singers—a more accessible name, considering "von" was not a big help during World War II—and started them on a series of concert tours that would bring them fame and accolades from coast to coast.

In addition to their undeniable talent, the Trapp Family Singers were lucky in that their American concert tours coincided with a new nationwide fascination with folk music and the way that it broke down the wall between highbrow and popular culture in America. American audiences also sympathized with the von Trapps as a group of refugees who had made something of their lives in their new country, and celebrated their endangered culture by singing about it. By 1944, the von Trapps had become as acclimatized as possible in America; with their first $1,000 in profit they bought a farm in the ski country of Stowe, Vermont, and began extensive renovations. Maria and the children also formally applied to become United States citizens. Perhaps most indicative of their new status as

PAGE 52: *Mary Martin perched atop a steamer trunk in Cole Porter's* Leave It To Me! *The particularly glowing chorus boy to her right is Gene Kelly, in his first Broadway show.*

PAGES 54–55: *In a more domestic role, Martin prepares the children for the Act One party.*

RIGHT: *The rechristened Trapp Family Singers on a 1946 tour to San Francisco. The group's resident musical genius, Father Wasner, is seated in front of the tour bus, to the left of Georg von Trapp.*

Town Hall

2 SUNDAY AFTERNOONS at 3.00
DEC. 14th and 21st

2 Xmas Carol Concerts 2

by the

TRAPP FAMILY SINGERS

DR. F. WASNER, Conductor

(PROGRAM OVERLEAF)

Americans, they became, as Schang had hoped, a commercial success. The Trapp Family Singers were Columbia's most successful choral group, averaging more than a hundred concerts a year during the war, and averaging fees of $1,000 per concert.

Both families and performing groups grow and change, and a performing family might well evolve more than most. When the war was over, the von Trapps grew in unexpected directions. The family was offered the chance to move back into their villa in Aigen but during the war it been had commandeered by Heinrich Himmler, the head of the nefarious Gestapo, who had turned it into a mini-fortress. Best to let it go, thought the von Trapps, and they sold it to a religious group, St. Joseph's Seminary, who control the estate to this very day. Some of the children decided to move on to other professions or start families of their own, and so the Family Singers, with the help of the inestimable Father Wasner, altered the vocal arrangements and brought in new recruits, including the three youngest children. Then, on May 30, 1947, the family suffered its greatest loss to date—the death of their dear patriarch, Georg von Trapp. He was interred on the Stowe estate, buried with the regimental flag of his submarine command that meant so much to him.

The Trapp Family Singers persevered, in various incarnations, for nearly another decade, touring three seasons a year, then summering at their home in Vermont, which they had turned into a massive Alpine chalet and resort lodge. One thing that had always made the von Trapps distinct from other vocal groups was the depth of their religious devotion. After a tour to Australia and New Zealand, Maria began to see that there was a higher purpose in life: "we thought our work had come to an end, [and then] we began to see a new beginning," wrote Maria in her memoirs. Exhausted after nearly two decades of touring and trying to hold an expanding family together, Maria heeded the call of a Catholic charity in New Guinea and disbanded the Trapp Family Singers after their 1955 tour. She, Father Wasner, and three of the children devoted themselves to God full-time and became missionaries on the other side of the world.

The saga of the Trapp Family Singers might well have ended there, leaving behind as their only cultural legacy a few long-playing albums of their repertoire and some happy memories in the hearts of a few hundred concertgoers. But, in 1948, Maria von Trapp was commissioned by an American publisher to recount the saga of her journey to America with her talented family. *The Story of the Trapp Family Singers* became a bestseller and its appeal did not go unnoticed.

During the twenty years that the von Trapps had performed in America, much had changed in the country's cultural landscape. There had been several musical revolutions, such as bebop and rock 'n' roll, although the Trapps' repertoire would have kept them far above the fray. One of the greatest evolutions in form was visited upon the world of musical comedy. Beginning in 1943, an influential style of musical narrative took over the world of Broadway. Thanks to the pioneering efforts of Richard Rodgers and Oscar Hammerstein II in *Oklahoma!*, a show's story would become the most important guiding principle of the musical rather than its stars, songs, or dance numbers. One might still encounter a throwaway musical number such as "My Heart Belongs to Daddy," but that kind of moment was getting rarer and rarer, thanks in no small part to the standards promoted by Rodgers and Hammerstein in subsequent shows such as *Carousel* and *The King and I*. By the end of the 1950s, the shows of Rodgers and Hammerstein were not only the most critically acclaimed of Broadway musicals, but the style of their shows became the dominant theatrical form for musicals around the world.

The focus on musical narrative challenged Rodgers and Hammerstein's peers to produce ever more sophisticated work. In 1943, Mary Martin herself returned to Broadway after a brief sojourn in Hollywood to star as a goddess thrust into wartime Manhattan in *One Touch of Venus*, scored by another émigré who had escaped Hitler, the German composer Kurt Weill. A decade later, she played the ageless sprite in a musical version of *Peter Pan*, which

LEFT: The Trapp Family Singers' career continued after World War II and they made sure to portray both their family and religious traditions in their advertisements.

was subsequently restaged for network television to huge acclaim. But her greatest success of this period came when she joined Rodgers and Hammerstein in 1949 as the heroine for their groundbreaking look at romance and racial prejudice in *South Pacific*. Martin's uncloying innocence was thrown a complex challenge when her all-American, corn-fed character is forced to confront the depths of her own racial prejudice. The musical was nearly as great a success as *Oklahoma!*, running 1,925 performances and, for her efforts, Martin was awarded the Tony for Best Actress in a Musical.

Martin had known, revered, and adored Oscar Hammerstein II since her early Hollywood stint in the 1930s, and *South Pacific* only cemented her mutual lovefest with, as she referred to them, Dick and Oscar. As friends and colleagues, the three were eager to work together again at some point. By the late 1950s, Martin was sorely in need of a successful project; a European tour and American revival of Thornton Wilder's *The Skin of Our Teeth* in which she starred had crash-landed on Broadway. She and her husband/manager Richard Halliday let the word go out that Mary Martin would indeed be interested in returning to the musical stage—if the project were attuned to the sensibilities of a musical-comedy leading lady in her early forties, and if it could be up to the standards of Rodgers and Hammerstein, so much the better.

Vincent J. Donehue was a friend and colleague of Martin's and a Tony-winning director. In the late 1950s, he was under contract to Paramount to develop projects for the movies and television. One day, Donehue had an appointment to look through various properties owned by Paramount to see if anything might be made of them. He was shown two German movies based on the memoirs of the Baroness Maria von Trapp; they were called *Die Trapp Familie* and its sequel *Die Trapp Familie in Amerika*. Neither movie had been released in America, but they were quite successful in Europe, and Paramount wondered if an English-language remake could be made out of them, maybe as a vehicle for Audrey Hepburn. Donehue

thought the story of the von Trapps would indeed make an excellent vehicle, but not for Hepburn and not for the movies; he went back to the East Coast and promptly screened the movies for Mary Martin and Richard Halliday.

It was exactly the kind of vehicle that the Hallidays had been searching for. They set about trying to contact Maria von Trapp's agent to make her an offer for the stage rights to her story, but they had no way of knowing that Maria had essentially renounced show business and was now deeply engaged in performing missionary work in, of all places, the South Pacific. Maria and Father Wasner were working in various jungle missions and every time they checked in at a major mission station there was a letter from two people named Martin and Halliday in America about something called a Broadway show. She simply tore up the letters and concentrated on her chosen vocation.

Months later, Maria and Father Wasner returned to the United States by ship and docked in San Francisco. Astonishingly, they were met there by Richard Halliday and were given two tickets to see Mary Martin at the Curran Theater in a touring production of *Annie Get Your Gun*. What a change of pace from Papua, New Guinea! Maria was impressed by Martin's talent, but could no more see Martin playing her than she could picture herself going onstage and singing about target shooting. She confessed to the couple that she had negotiated away the stage and screen rights to the German producers of *Die Trapp Familie* for the paltry sum of $9,000. She told the Hallidays that they were welcome to give it a go, but she herself had more important work to do and returned to the family lodge in Vermont.

The Hallidays were extremely close to Broadway producer Leland Hayward, a former agent who had been equally successful with serious dramas, such as *A Bell For Adano*, and musical comedies, such as Ethel Merman's *Call Me Madam*. Hayward also had a huge success as a co-producer on *South Pacific*. It was there that he began his professional collaboration with Martin and went on to work with her on *Peter Pan* as well as on an extremely popular television "spectacular" starring Martin and Merman, Martin's only contemporary rival for Broadway fame.

RIGHT: Leland Hayward's producing powers were more well-known than his piano-playing abilities, but that didn't stop a publicist from wrangling a snapshot with Mary Martin astride a baby grand.

LEFT: "The Beamish Ones," they were dubbed by Boris Karloff. Howard Lindsay (left) and Russel Crouse, two of Broadway's most revered and respected craftsmen, producers, and pranksters. Here, they compare notes during the Boston tryout.

ABOVE: To everyone on Broadway, they were known as "Dick and Oscar"; the millions of fans around the world knew them as Rodgers and Hammerstein.

The Hallidays presented their dilemma to Hayward; they had found the perfect property for Martin's next starring vehicle, but the German producers were proving intractable—and expensive.

Hayward thought it was a great idea and happily agreed to coproduce the show. He dispatched his lawyer to Munich to secure the rights, but it took six trips across the Atlantic before a deal could be signed. In a gesture of generosity rare for Broadway producers, Hayward gave Maria von Trapp a small percentage—three-eighths of one percent—of the eventual royalties. With the rights successfully secured, Hayward turned to his next creative challenge: figuring out who would write the show. At this point, he envisioned the stage version as a straight play with occasional songs from the Trapps' own repertoire.

Hayward's choice for the script were two gentlemen who had been Broadway fixtures for nearly a quarter of a century: Howard Lindsay and Russel "Buck" Crouse. In 1934, Lindsay, a director and actor, had been handed the plum assignment of staging the latest Cole Porter musical, a shipboard escapade starring Ethel Merman. The original book was such a mess that the producer begged Lindsay to take it over. Lindsay himself was overwhelmed and turned to Crouse, then a press agent for the Theater Guild. Friends had recommended Crouse as one smart cookie, which was what the musical—eventually called *Anything Goes*—needed. Lindsay and Crouse conducted a major rewrite and turned the incipient disaster into one of the great hits of the 1930s.

Lindsay and Crouse continued their partnership, writing a series of musical-comedy librettos such as *Red, Hot and Blue* and *Call Me Madam* or pertinent political plays, such as *State of the Union* (which won them the Pulitzer Prize). Lindsay and Crouse became savvy producers as well, with two of the biggest smash-hit comedies of the 1940s: *Life With Father* (which they also wrote and in which Lindsay starred) and *Arsenic and Old Lace* (for which they provided major rewriting). In addition, they became beloved along Broadway as first-class pranksters and practical jokers. No one wrote funnier opening-night telegrams than Lindsay and Crouse. Crouse's wife-to-be, Anna, described them thus in a 1941 piece for the *Herald Tribune*:

They couldn't be more unalike. For instance, Lindsay answers all his mail, including insurance and haberdashery advertisements. Crouse answers nothing, leaves everything on his desk, except for precious odds and ends which he files in his pockets. This file includes addresses, grocery bills, jottings on future plays and sometimes even a check for $20,000, which he has been carrying in his pocket for five months.

Lindsay and Crouse hardly seemed like natural choices for a devotional play about Austrian folksingers, but Hayward—also their agent—had known them for years and had produced several of their smash hits. He knew them to represent the pinnacle of Broadway craftsmanship. He even offered them two other projects: a musical version of *Gone with the Wind*, or a musical version of the memoirs of Gypsy Rose Lee. (The latter, of course, went on to become the legendary *Gypsy* in other hands.) But Lindsay and Crouse far preferred the Trapp Family project.

As Lindsay and Crouse began assembling the material, Hayward felt that the traditional musical selections of the von Trapps should be augmented by some new Broadway material—and approached his old *South Pacific* colleagues Rodgers and Hammerstein. The songwriters liked the material, but competing with Mozart, Haydn, and Pergolesi was not their cup of tea. "[That idea] seemed to me most impractical," said Rodgers in a *New York Times* interview. "Either you do it authentically—all actual Trapp music—or you get a complete new score for it." In any event, a new score from Rodgers and Hammerstein would be a long time in coming—they were contracted to start on their next show, *Flower Drum Song*, which was scheduled to go into rehearsal by September 1958. "Then," Rodgers continued, the producers and Lindsay and Crouse said "the most flattering thing in the world—'If you and Oscar will write the music and lyrics, we will wait.'"

And so they did. This respite gave Lindsay and Crouse nearly a year to break down the epic saga of the Trapp family's wanderings into something manageable for the musical stage. They made the decision to begin their story at Nonnberg Abbey, where Maria, with her tomboyish ebullience, is quickly revealed to be an impossible fit for the novitiate. Interestingly, the story concluded not back at Nonnberg Abbey with the departure of the Trapp family to America, but in America itself, at the detention center on Ellis Island. Lindsay and Crouse had highlighted the show-business aspect of the

"I WAS BORN IN TEXAS AND SHE WAS BORN IN AUSTRIA,
BUT UNDERNEATH, WE WERE THE SAME MARIA."
MARY MARTIN

ABOVE: *The real Maria and her first interpreter: Prior to the show's going
into rehearsal in the fall of 1959, Mary Martin spent two weeks in
Vermont with her role model.*

THE SOUND OF MUSIC

Tentative routine of songs:
(mostly "dummy" titles)

Chorale, A Capella   Female Choir (Recorded)

✓ The Sound of Music   Maria   ✗
✓ *MARIA*
Sad Song   *SISTER*
Happy Song   Maria   ✓

✓ First Singing Lesson   Maria and Children   ✗

Duet   (Young lovers)   "Balkans?"   ✓

✓ Yodeling Song   (To drown out thunder) Maria, Children   ✗
                                                        (Frau Schmidt)
                                                                                 ✓

"Sophisticated Love Song"   Captain and Elsa

The Sound of Music   Reprise   Children
    (Developed Chorally and as "Step out")

~~I'm a Little Out Of Breath~~   ~~Captain and Maria~~

Waltz, opening to scene   Captain, Elsa and
    (Reprise "Sophisticated?)   Ensemble

Children's Farewell Song   Children

"Face Life"   Abbess to and with Maria

ACT TWO

"Why Buck The Tide?"   Elsa, Max and Captain

Maria's Return (Yodel?)   Maria and Children

When Not To Tell The Truth   Captain to small child

I've Been In Love Before   Captain, to Maria
    (So I know what I'm saying)

Love Is Not Blind   Maria and Nuns

Chorale (Wedding Service) off-stage   Nuns
    counter to Nun's comments through grille

Song for one or both of young lovers

Concert Song (Development of "First
    Singing Lesson?)   Maria, Captain and Children
Reprise of "Farewell"

Finale (Reprise "Face Life")   Others, Nuns, Trapp Family

tale, introducing a fictional American concert manager for the von Trapps, who gets the immigration authorities on Ellis Island to release Maria after they hear how wonderfully she can sing. It is not the promise of America, but rather, the promise of an American stage debut, that provided the dramatic climax for the initial draft of the show.

Lindsay and Crouse hewed essentially to the dramatic arc of Maria's memoirs, but the stage requires a certain condensation and conflation with any large narrative. The Captain and Maria marry each other late in the dramatic version, and their honeymoon is depicted as nearly simultaneous with the beginning of the *Anschluss*. In reality, of course, those two events were more than a decade apart. Within those years, the major events of the von Trapp family revolved around the birth of Rosmarie and Eleonore; once those years were conflated, the two girls (and by extension, Johannes) vanished with them. In what was surely a greater affront to the von Trapp children than to Austrian history, however, all of the children's names were changed (into rather operetta-like names), as well as their ages and their sexes. Also, for the record, Maria Kutschera herself is renamed—in the show she becomes Maria Rainer, perhaps in a tribute to the Austrian-trained movie actress Luise Rainer.

This was the general tenor of the material in early spring 1959, when Rodgers and Hammerstein received the onion-skin manuscript of "Trapp Family," as it was then called, from Lindsay and Crouse—their third draft of the material. The next task was for the four collaborators to break down the narrative and transform key text passages into songs that could heighten the story and allow it to achieve its maximum dramatic potential. Lindsay and Crouse met constantly with the songwriters, and planned every turn of the musical narrative in collaboration with them. There were no songwriters better at this than Rodgers and Hammerstein, who took dialogue from Lindsay and Crouse and recast it as songs ("Maria"), and when Lindsay and Crouse came to them with problems in streamlining the story, Rodgers and Hammerstein were able to craft songs to move the narrative along. For example, in Act Two, Lindsay and Crouse needed an emotional shift in the story when the Captain sets aside his affections for Elsa—who has broken

off their engagement—and then admits his love for Maria, so Rodgers and Hammerstein provided "An Ordinary Couple," a romantic duet that neatly provided the perfect resolution to a dramatically efficient and effective scene. First, however, Rodgers and Hammerstein worked out the routine of the songs—the structure of how musical material would alternate between solos and group numbers, up-tempo songs and ballads—everything to create a satisfying harmony and balance in the show. An early tentative routine of songs in outline form shows how close Rodgers and Hammerstein got to the final form of the show, acting only on intuition and talent.

Rodgers and Hammerstein did make one major structural change in Lindsay and Crouse's second draft. Originally the intermission was to come after Scene Eight, where Maria sneaks off from the Captain's party, guitar and satchel in hand, heartbroken but determined to return to the Abbey. Rodgers and Hammerstein wanted the Act One curtain to come down on a song they would write, preferably an uplifting one, so they asked Lindsay and Crouse to move the Act One curtain one scene later, after Maria returns to the Abbey and is given spiritual advice by the Mother Abbess. "You have to face life, wherever you are," was the final line that Lindsay and Crouse typed for the Mother Abbess—but in their script, in blue ink, the merry pranksters scrawled underneath, "At this point she also has to face Rodgers and Hammerstein."

Rodgers and Hammerstein were about to have some spiritual guidance of their own. Hammerstein began a correspondence with a friend of the Hallidays, Sister Gregory, a nun who served as head of the drama department at Rosary College in River Forest, Illinois. The sister became an unofficial technical advisor in Catholic matters and soon became a much-needed spiritual advisor as well. Sister Gregory's inspirational letters fed Hammerstein's expansive soul, and as the collaboration on *The Sound of Music* grew, his lyrics took on a quality that was more yearning, more compelling, and more spiritually challenging.

Rodgers, for his part, was introduced to Mother Morgan at College of the Sacred Heart in Westchester County, New York. It was she who invited Rodgers to

several concerts of Catholic liturgical music and was willing to answer any questions he might have about devotional hymns, Gregorian chants, polyphony, and so on. This is the closest Rodgers ever got to musicological research for any project; his pure intuitive musicianship usually made the songs sound effortlessly like one-part Tin Pan Alley, one-part Oklahoman folk songs, or Siamese court music, or liturgical texts. But he was grateful for his informative visit to Sacred Heart. In fact, *The Sound of Music* contains some of his most effective pastiches; the "Laendler" folk dance that brings the Captain and Maria together for the first time, with its faint inversion of "The Lonely Goatherd," sounds for all the world like a pure native Austrian tune. Rodgers was lucky in that his loyal vocal and dance arranger, Trude Rittman, was also a German émigré and could supply the proper grace notes to the score.

One last bit of advice came from someone with even more at stake. Maria von Trapp had read an early draft of the script and had three main concerns: she felt that the character of Maria was not enough of a tomboy and therefore did not undergo enough of a change; second, the Captain was far too Prussian and humorless than the real item. But most importantly, how could the creators possibly eliminate Father Wasner, the one person most responsible for the professional success of the Trapp Family Singers? Lindsay and Crouse had warned her early on that the show could contain either Father Wasner or Mary Martin, but not both—either a priest could teach the children to sing, or the star could. Most of Maria's comments were astute, but Richard Halliday, perhaps wisely, did whatever he could to keep the headstrong matriarch back home in Vermont during rehearsals. There was one last thing that needed fixing: the title. Originally called *Love Song*, the show was changed to *The Sound of Music* when Rodgers and Hammerstein's lawyer found dozens of copyrighted shows bearing the former title and begged them to use something less susceptible to a plagiarism lawsuit.

By the last week of August 1959—little more than half a year after the collaboration had begun—the show had been shaped enough to go into rehearsals. Casting had proceeded without incident. Martin, of course, would play Maria and participated in all major casting decisions. The producers and director Vincent Donehue sought New York's most handsome leading men for the part of Captain von Trapp (including, rumor has it, a Canadian classical actor named

ABOVE: Richard Rodgers and his wife Dorothy attend a concert of religious music; it was to be a profitable research trip.

RIGHT: Richard Rodgers plays the score to The Sound of Music to Richard Halliday (above Rodgers). To his left are Theodore Bikel, Mary Martin, and Oscar Hammerstein.

Christopher Plummer, who was deemed too young). Theodore Bikel was Viennese-born, and, in addition to his acting career, had an impressive sideline as a folksinger. When, after performing some more typical Broadway tunes, he brought his guitar and accompanied himself on a folk song, he sealed the deal with Martin immediately. "We don't have to look anywhere else, do we?" she asked Rodgers. Rounding out the cast in two parts invented just for the show were Marion Marlowe as Elsa Schraeder, a worldly, aristocratic love interest for the Captain, and the ever-engaging character actor Kurt Kasznar as Max Detweiler, the cynical impresario who encourages the family to perform at the Salzburg Festival (although that was changed, too—perhaps for reasons of propriety—to the Kaltzberg Festival). On the production side of the team were scenic designer Oliver Smith, costumer Lucinda Ballard, and choreographer Joe Layton, who would be in charge of the many musical staging sequences involving the seven von Trapp children. In the category of "Only on Broadway," Martin's simple frocks and dresses would be created by the haute couture designer Mainbocher, who had transformed Martin into a goddess for *One Touch of Venus* in 1943. Everything seemed to be, as befits a show starring a submarine commander, shipshape.

But then, after the third week of rehearsal, Oscar Hammerstein went in for a routine physical with his physician and discovered he had cancer of the stomach. An operation was immediately scheduled for mid-September. It was partially successful—the carcinoma had been removed, but so had most of his stomach. Hammerstein could still function, but he would miss both the final run-throughs in New York and the out-of-town engagement in New Haven, Connecticut, in early October. A showbiz trouper since his twenties, it would be the first time that the hands-on Hammerstein would miss the crucial rehearsals and tryouts of a new project. "We are going to work as long as we can," said Rodgers, himself a cancer survivor, in an attempt to comfort Mary Martin, according to Max Wilk's *Overture and Finale*. In a missive from Rosary College, Sister Gregory gently chided Hammerstein for "chickening out" of the New Haven tryout, but when the Hallidays soon told her the real reason for Hammerstein's absence, she wrote Hammerstein and his wife a contrite letter: "It's the worst possible time for Mr. Hammerstein to be 'benched' . . . but seems to me that when we are working with others, as you two most certainly are, we must have a core of peace, a secret place within, a place strictly our own where we can retire to be refreshed, to think, and grow." Lindsay and Crouse cabled to Hammerstein a more characteristic telegram from New Haven: "WE ARE SIXTY, GOING ON 70, YOU CAN DEPEND ON US. HOWARD AND BUCK."

Despite the absence of Hammerstein, the week long New Haven tryout went without hitch on the creative front (although Patricia Neway as the Mother Abbess missed a few performances due to illness) and the show garnered the sort of acclaim that usually accompanied a Rodgers and Hammerstein musical at the Shubert Theater. Hammerstein was able to join the company halfway through the two-week Boston engagement and, although still recovering, he enthusiastically gave notes on the performance and the show. Very little needed to be fixed; it was the threat of the *Anschluss* and the appearance of the Nazis in the second act that most needed strengthening. Even in 1959, fifteen years after the end of the war, it was not that common to see Nazis on stage in a Broadway show. *The Sound of Music* was the first time that Nazis—in a serious incarnation—had ever appeared in a Broadway musical. Tact was required and the physical presence of Nazi officers was played down as the show was revised, utilizing more insinuation than brutality. "The end result," said Rodgers to the *New York Times*, "is that there's more menace without seeing them than there was on stage in those musical comedy uniforms—after all, who are we going to offend, people who like Nazis?"

Opening night at Broadway's Lunt-Fontanne Theater came on November 16, 1959. The show had cost $400,000—a not insignificant sum back then—but it also had $2,320,000 advance sale, a record for its time. The opening of a Rodgers and Hammerstein musical was a biennial event, and still one of the most anticipated evenings on Broadway. Although most of the Boston reviews were raves, the astute local critic Elliot Norton had set the creative team on edge with his cavils about the show's "silliness, stiffness and corny operetta falseness of the script." Still, none of this mattered to the opening-night crowd in New York, who applauded mightily after the final curtain came down. When Mary Martin came forward to take her curtain call, a formidable gray-haired woman in a green satin dress stood up immediately and applauded. Martin was not shocked—the same woman had stood up at precisely the same moment during the opening nights in New Haven and Boston. Besides, Martin had sent her the green dress as an opening-night present. Mary Martin bowed, looked at the woman, and blew her a grateful kiss. Why shouldn't she? After all, *The Sound of Music* was the story of the woman in the green dress. And, as the previous three hours made abundantly clear, one couldn't tell Maria von Trapp what to do.

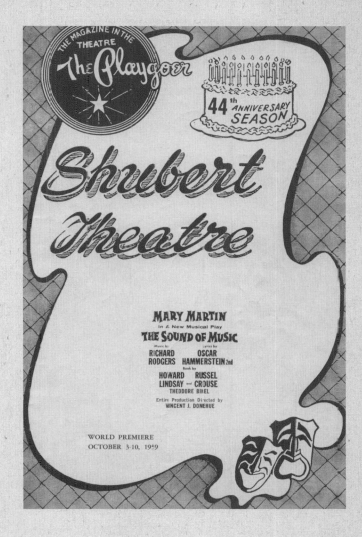

LEFT: Mary Martin makes friends with the children on Oliver Smith's two-tiered set.

ABOVE: "When a Rodgers and Hammerstein show hit New Haven, it was always in pretty good shape," said theater historian Max Wilk. Here is the program cover for the world premiere engagement of The Sound of Music.

THE SOUND OF MUSIC

My day in the hills
Has come to an end, I know.
A star has come out
To tell me it's time to go,
But deep in the dark-green shadows
Are voices that urge me to stay.
So I pause and I wait and I listen
For one more sound,
For one more lovely thing
That the hills might say . . .

The hills are alive
With the sound of music,
With songs they have sung
For a thousand years.
The hills fill my heart
With the sound of music
My heart wants to sing
Every song it hears.

My heart wants to beat
Like the wings
Of the birds that rise
From the lake to the trees.
My heart wants to sigh
Like a chime that flies
From a church on a breeze,
To laugh like a brook
When it trips and falls
Over stones in its way,
To sing through the night
Like a lark who is learning to pray—

I go to the hills
When my heart is lonely,
I know I will hear
What I've heard before.
My heart will be blessed
With the sound of music
And I'll sing once more.

"When you sing, you pray twice." This was a common saying among the von Trapp family, and whether or not Oscar Hammerstein knew of it, he certainly turned its philosophy into the essential core of this song.

Although technically not the first number in the Broadway show (that would be the nuns' "Preludium"), "The Sound of Music" is, to all intent and purposes, the defining song of the piece. It is also the title number, which carries with it a special responsibility; in all of Rodgers and Hammerstein's shows, only three—*Oklahoma!*, *Allegro*, and *The Sound of Music*—have title numbers, and each song has a special significance to the story. Hammerstein was famous for saying that the first ten minutes of any musical-theater piece should define the style and the themes to follow. In "The Sound of Music," he sets up not only the style and theme but some essential plot points as well.

To begin with, Hammerstein has Maria associate music with spirituality; her love of music and her faith are inseparable. In an early draft of the lyrics, he created a sense of yearning in Maria, eager to be fulfilled by something she has not yet experienced. Hammerstein also knew early on that this would be the song reprised by the children in the middle of the first act. And the word that appears most in the stage lyrics—"hills"—sets up Maria's affinity for and knowledge of the hills surrounding Salzburg (something the real Maria did not have). This presages an important plot point at the climax of the show, when Maria must use her knowledge of the hills to lead her family out of Salzburg and into safety.

In the Broadway version, Mary Martin as Maria is discovered in the branches of a tree. In Max Wilk's *Overture and Finale*, Lauri Peters (the original Liesl) is quoted as saying, "When she appeared in that tree at the opening . . . she was reaching out to [the audience] and they immediately reached back. People got chills." Early in rehearsals, Martin's husband, coproducer Richard Halliday, had the idea that it might be cute if Martin got her bloomers caught in a tree branch on her way down. When approached with the idea,

Rodgers and Hammerstein demurred—it did not seem to be the right moment in the show for underpants humor. Theater historian Ethan Mordden, in his survey of Rodgers and Hammerstein's career, recounted that Halliday was furious with the rejection of his idea. "You know what your problem is," Halliday supposedly shouted to the songwriting team, "all you guys care about is the show."

In the movie version, director Robert Wise and screenwriter Ernest Lehman cleverly began the movie smack-dab in the middle of the song and created one of the most legendary openings in screen history. In order to start with a bang (or a swirl, at any rate), the introductory verse was cut, although some of its music is heard in Maria's next solo, "Have Confidence." Wise used his editing sleight of hand to make it seem as if it is one long aerial zoom into Maria on top of the hill, when in fact, it is a very skillful cut. Getting the shot itself proved to be one of the most complicated efforts of the entire location shoot. The "hill" is a mountain called Mellweg, near a village in Bavaria, about eight miles from Salzburg. The opening was actually the last location shot in the picture and inclement weather kept Julie Andrews, Wise, and the crew at Mellweg for several days waiting for the clouds to break. Richard Zanuck, the Fox studio chief, was begging Wise to bring his crew back to Los Angeles in order to keep the production schedule on track, but Wise dug his heels in and waited it out. A gutsy move—where would the movie be without that shot?

However, when the clouds broke, the difficulties were just beginning. According to Julie Andrews, interviewed for the fortieth anniversary DVD of *The Sound of Music*:

> You could say that that opening shot of my coming across the fields at the beginning of the film is really the quintessential postcard picture . . . but it was a very difficult shot to get. I would start at one end of the field and a huge helicopter with a very brave cameraman hanging out the side of it would start at the other end of the field and he would swoop down

PAGE 73: *Maurice Zuberano's watercolor storyboards set up one of the most famous establishing shots in movie history.*

RIGHT: *Someone in a tree: Mary Martin makes her first appearance—but not on a hill!*

THE SOUND OF MUSIC

I HEAR THE ECHO OF A FAR OFF CHIME
AS IT FLIES (Floats)
          FROM A CHURCH
                    ON A BREEZE.   *the wings of*
I HEAR THE CLATTER OF A CLOUD OF BIRDS   *wild birds were*
AS THEY RISE   *movers*
          FROM THE LAKE
                    TO THE TREES.

     TO-DAY, THE SKY IS FILLED WITH MUSIC,
     THE SOUND OF MUSIC,
     OF SUMMER MUSIC,
     AND WHEN THE SKY IS FILLED WITH MUSIC,
     MY HEART WANTS TO SING EVERY SONG IT HEARS.

                      Bom bird calls
A DOG IS BARKING AND A SCHOOLBOY SHOUTS   *I hear the laughter of a*
AS HE SWINGS   *as he snaps*   *the laughter of a happy child*
     ON THE BRANCH   *on the rocks*   *of a pine*
          (loosely)   OF A PINE.
A BROOK IS SINGING ON ITS WAY TO SEA
WITH A FAITH
          THAT I WISH
               COULD BE MINE.

     TO-DAY, THE EARTH IS FILLED WITH MUSIC,   *Brook:*
     THE SOUND OF MUSIC,
     UNWRITTEN MUSIC,   *The and sounds of summer are*
     THE SOUNDS OF SUMMER ON A HILLSIDE
     WILL STILL BE THE SAME IN A THOUSAND YEARS.

I HEAR A SILENCE AT THE END OF DAY
WHEN THE SUN
          FINDS A HILL   AND DEPARTS.   *a low*
     AND IN THE SILENCE YOU CAN HEAR A SOUND   *whisper*
     LIKE THE BEAT OF A FEW MILLION HEARTS... *THE FOREST IS SWEE* 'LOW THROB'
AND NOW THE NIGHT IS FILLED WITH MUSIC,   *a whispered so*
THE SOUND OF MUSIC,
OF STARLIGHT MUSIC,
AND WHEN THE NIGHT IS FILLED WITH MUSIC
MY HEART WANTS TO SING
MY HEART WANTS TO SING   *Like the beating*
MY HEART WANTS TO SING EVERY SONG IT HEARS!   *of millions of hearts*

The music swells. The lights are
dimming slowly from the orange of
sunset to the blue of evening.
MARIA can perhaps hear an echo of
the singing from the convent, but
the singing is low, suggesting that
the convent is some distance off.
A look of concern comes over her
face, she balances herself on the
branch as if preparing to climb
down. Then she hears a bird call.
She rests back on the branch of the
tree and looks up and smiles. The
voices from the convent are heard
again. She looks off in their
direction, and now she starts to
sing:)

                    Maria

My day in the hills
Has come to an end I know.
A star has come out
To tell me it's time to go,
But deep in the dark green shadows
Are voices that urge me to stay.
So I pause and I wait and I listen
For one more sound,
For one more lovely thing
That the hills might say ....

The hills are alive
With the sound of music,
With songs they have sung
For a thousand years.
The hills fill my heart
With the sound of music
And my heart wants to sing
Every song it hears.
          My heart/wants to beat
          Like the wings of the birds
          That rise from the lake to the trees.
          My heart wants to sigh
          Like the tones of a chime
          That float from a church on a breeze,
          To laugh like a brook
          When it trips on a stone,   *Tripping on stone*   *on/all*
          To hum like the leaves on the vines,   *over stone a it say*
          To play in the dark   *To sing through the mists*
          Like a nightingale,   *Like*
          To sing through a storm like the pines --
   I go to The hills give me strength
          When my heart is lonely
   I know I And lost in the fog   *will have*
   will give Of a thousand fears.   *heart before*
          The hills fill my heart   *will be back*
          With the sound of music
          And my heart wants to sing.   *and I'll sing once more.*

                                        (Continue

---

through the trees . . . and I would walk towards it, we'd get closer and closer to each other, then I would make that big turn just before singing, and that was the end of that particular shot. . . . The only thing is that the downdraft from the helicopter engine was so strong that every time he went around me to go back to the end of the field, he absolutely flattened me into the ground. . . . I finally tried to signal to the helicopter pilot could he please make a wider turn around me, and all I got was this thumbs-up and you know, "Doing great, just keep it up."

ABOVE LEFT: *Oscar Hammerstein's early drafts show him searching for the right poetry to convey Maria's yearning. The "summer music" would give way to something less specific, but the chimes of the church and flight of the birds would remain in another form.*

Some other bits of Hollywood trickery helped the opening number: both the mini-orchard of birch trees and the brook used for skipping stones were added by the production designer (a neighboring farmer took such umbrage at the crew's presence that he damaged the basin for the brook with his pitchfork). Speaking of brooks, one last change from the stage version: in Hammerstein's manuscript, one can clearly see that his brook "trips and falls / Over stones in its way," not "*on* its way," as is sung in the movie.

ABOVE RIGHT: *Last-minute tinkering. For Hammerstein, every word counted and by changing the last line, he propelled Maria's story forward.*

RIGHT: *Julie Andrews rehearsing that famous shot: gamely waiting for one more pass by that menacing helicopter, no doubt.*

CHAPTER FOUR

BROADWAY TO HOLLYWOOD

When a Broadway musical is successful, the producers waste little time in mounting a second production to tour the country. Rodgers and Hammerstein were expert at this sort of thing as well, founding their own production company in the mid-1940s in order to keep various tours, foreign productions, and replacement casts under their own control. *The Sound of Music* assembled its first national touring company in February 1961, while the show was still running on Broadway. Florence Henderson, who made her Broadway debut in 1953, was cast as Maria. Henderson, at the age of twenty-six, would be the first actress to play Maria at something close to Maria von Trapp's actual age during the events of the musical.

The touring company would eventually make its debut in Detroit, but a final run-through was put together on the stage of the Lunt-Fontanne, on a Sunday when the show wasn't performing, so that the Broadway cast could watch the show. Mary Martin watched the performance with her fellow company members, rapt with attention, but during the intermission, she was, according to Anna Crouse, "on her hands and knees, feeling around the floor. Russel said, 'Mary, what's the matter?' and she said, 'I didn't know the show was this sad—and I cried out my contact lens!'"

Of course, all Martin had to do was think of her favorite things—as well as her twenty-five percent investment in the production—and then she wouldn't feel so bad, but the years immediately following the opening of *The Sound of Music* brought tears of joy, tears of frustration, tears of sorrow, and tears of exhaustion.

"IT IS CURIOUS THAT THE PLAY RUNNING IN NEW YORK
THIS SEASON TO THE GREATEST NUMBER OF PEOPLE
IS CONCERNED WITH A YOUNG CATHOLIC ABOUT
TO BECOME A NUN AND HER FRIENDS.
SOMEBODY DOWN HERE LIKES US." RICHARD RODGERS

PAGE 78: *Here's the story of a lovely lady: More than a decade before her debut as a famous TV mom in* The Brady Bunch, *Florence Henderson was the accomplished leading musical actress who took* The Sound of Music *on tour.*

PAGES 80–81: *How sweet it is! Mary Martin displays her fourth Tony Award for Best Actress in a Musical, next to Jackie Gleason, who won for* Take Me Along. *Sharing the honors on the dramatic side during the 1960 awards ceremony are Anne Bancroft (*The Miracle Worker*) and Melvyn Douglas (*The Best Man*).*

ABOVE: *Martin and Rodgers during the recording of the original cast album by Columbia Records: the eventual release would stay on the billboard charts for more than five years.*

First, the tears of frustration: the reviews. In New Haven and Boston, *The Sound of Music* had received enthusiastic reviews, with the noted exception of Elliot Norton. This stung, as Rodgers and Hammerstein had great respect for Norton. They also had respect for Brooks Atkinson of the *New York Times* and Walter Kerr of the *Herald Tribune*. The two were the most powerful critics in New York and, although most of their colleagues had exuberant praise for the score and the Lindsay and Crouse libretto, Atkinson and Kerr were not moved by the proceedings at the Lunt-Fontanne. Kerr wrote: "Before *The Sound of Music* is halfway through its promising chores, it becomes not only too sweet for words, but almost too sweet for music . . . the pitch is too strong; the taste of vanilla overwhelms the solid chocolate; the people onstage have all melted before our hearts do." Atkinson praised the craftsmanship of Rodgers and Hammerstein, but saved his whammy for the conclusion: ". . . the scenario of *The Sound of Music* has the hackneyed look of the musical theater [Rodgers and Hammerstein] replaced with *Oklahoma!* in 1943 . . . It is disappointing to see the American musical stage succumbing to the clichés of operetta."

The term "operetta," with a pejorative implication, is one that cynical critics have tried to tack on to *The Sound of Music* since its inception and, actually, it is a rather inaccurate one. Operetta was, indeed, conceived and refined in Vienna around the middle of the eighteenth century, but very few of its conceits exist in *The Sound of Music*. Operettas tend to focus on male/female romance; here the great romance, as Maria von Trapp said, is between Maria and the children. Operettas allow the lead characters to indulge in vocal pyrotechnics; here, the leading man has one subtle duet with the leading lady and one solo, accompanying himself on guitar. Operettas usually exist in exotic or romanticized settings, not a villa or a convent. And operettas usually conclude with a contrived happy ending; persecution and exile hardly count.

Harsh, even vindictive, criticism would follow the show in its every incarnation over the next four-and-a-half decades. Some of it, to be fair, had to do with changing tastes in American culture. Rock 'n' roll had made its permanent presence known in popular music by 1959. Musical shows such as *West Side Story* and *Gypsy*—both of which were created by, among others, Jerome Robbins, Arthur Laurents, and Stephen Sondheim—showed Broadway audiences that there was room for more complicated and confrontational material in the modern musical. And a show that affirmed the values of family, faith, and freedom in America would be out of step with the unconventional drumbeat of the cultural revolution in the 1960s. *The Sound of Music* was one of the last important musicals to open in the 1950s, although both *Fiorello!* and *Once Upon a Mattress*, with a score by Rodgers' daughter Mary, would open on Broadway in the weeks following. Could one not simply say that *The Sound of Music* was a smash at the box office and leave it at that?

One could, but Rodgers and Hammerstein, who had done so much to revolutionize the American musical, were particularly nettled by any suggestions that their work was retrograde in any way. Rodgers, normally the more pugnacious of the duo, responded to these criticisms on July 10, 1960, seven months after the opening, in a *New York Times* piece celebrating Hammerstein's sixty-fifth birthday:

> Most of us still feel that nature can have attractive manifestations, that children aren't necessarily monsters and that deep affection between two people is nothing to be ashamed of . . . it is curious that the play running in New York this season to the greatest number of people and the largest amount of money, *The Sound of Music*, is concerned with a young Catholic about to become a nun and her friends. Somebody down here likes us.

Oscar uncharacteristically let loose in a letter to a colleague who had accused the team of looking for something "sure-fire" to star Martin:

> Mary Martin found this property first and then invited us into it. We accepted the invitation because we liked the story very much. . . . We didn't remember any other musical plays which dealt with the problems of a postulant who had made her mind to take the veil and then fall in love with a man. We thought it a very original situation that when her problem was put before the Mother Superior, that the Mother advised her to go back to the man. We, in our innocence, considered this a very original turn of plot and a situation of great human interest. . . . You see, the situation is even worse than you

thought. Not only have we concocted this syrupy musical play, but we all love it and it has turned out to be a great success. That does not mean you should endorse it or like it. Nor are we obliged to agree with you that it is unadulterated treacle.

Now, the tears of joy.

At the 1960 Tony Awards, *The Sound of Music* was nominated for nine Tonys and won six. The nominees included Theodore Bikel and Kurt Kasznar (both for Best Featured Actor); Vincent Donehue; and, in a distinction unmatched before or since, Lauri Peters and all the other Trapp children were nominated jointly as Best Featured Actress in a show. (Patricia Neway was also nominated in that category as the Mother Abbess, and won the Tony.) The set designer Oliver Smith won a Tony, as did Frederic Dvonch as conductor and musical director. Mary Martin picked up the fourth Tony of her career (the others being for the tour of *Annie Get Your Gun*, *Peter Pan*, and *South Pacific*) and there was some tension over her competition in this category with her chum, Ethel Merman, who had been nominated for the performance of her lifetime in *Gypsy*. Merman took the loss with equanimity: "How are you going to buck a nun?" she shrugged. *The Sound of Music* won the Tony for Best Musical, although, in another unprecedented vote, it tied with *Fiorello!*, a musical about New York's mayor, Fiorello La Guardia, who served as a captain in World War I, just like Georg von Trapp. Even though Rodgers won a Tony for Best Score, there was no award in 1960 for Best Lyrics.

A shame, because Hammerstein's time was running out. By the Tony Awards, Hammerstein knew that his cancer had returned and that he was dying. In late summer 1960, he retired to his farm in Doylestown, Pennsylvania, and waited for the inevitable, surrounded by family and friends. Hammerstein died on August 23. He was mourned in every major newspaper across America and in London and by all of his friends and colleagues who knew that, over a forty-year career, he had changed the face of the American theater. On September 1, the City of New York paid an

unprecedented tribute. All of Times Square—as opposed to the marquees of all the theaters, as was customary—would be blacked out for one minute at nine o'clock in the evening, just as the cast of *The Sound of Music*, still led by Mary Martin, would be getting close to singing "My Favorite Things." But Rodgers and the other producers had asked for no special memorial or tribute that night. They posted a note to this effect backstage: "If you give a performance comparable with last Tuesday [the day of his death]—it will be the best possible memorial for Mr. Hammerstein." In a tribute to Hammerstein's influence, London's theatrical circle paid the lyricist a similar honor five hours earlier by dimming the lights of the West End.

London had always admired Hammerstein, and he appreciated it enough to live there briefly in the 1930s. As early as 1926, he had enjoyed an unbelievably popular success with his book and lyrics to *Rose-Marie* at the Theatre Royal, Drury Lane. This began a string of hits for Hammerstein in the late 1920s as, one by one, his Broadway operettas conquered London, usually at the Drury Lane: *The Desert Song*, *Show Boat*, a revival of *Rose-Marie*, and *The New Moon*. When *Oklahoma!* opened at the Drury Lane in 1947, it began a second Hammerstein revolution with consecutive runs of *Carousel*, *South Pacific*, and *The King and I* that lasted nine years. A London production of *The Sound of Music* was inevitable—sadly, Hammerstein was not around to witness the show's immense success on the West End.

Of the top twenty-five longest-running musicals to open in London before 1961, Oscar Hammerstein had written four of them; *The Sound of Music* would make number five, and its popularity in London would eclipse all of his other projects there. Unlike Broadway, it would contain no stars; the Maria, Jean Bayless, was largely known through her television work. After the production opened in May 1961 at the Palace Theatre, the critical reaction was far worse than that to the New York version. W. A. Darlington of the *Daily Telegraph* wrote, "Take the basic story of *The King and I*, scrape the oriental spicing and substitute Austrian sugar-icing an inch thick. Add a little bit of drama

at the end." Rodgers and Lindsay and Crouse thought they had been dealt a huge failure at the box office, but audiences felt otherwise. By the time it would close in London in 1967 *The Sound of Music* would rack up 2,386 performances, nearly 1,000 more than its Broadway counterpart. Perhaps its success was due to the fact that so many London families—much like the von Trapps—had suffered because of the Nazis, or that so many of the children who had been separated from their parents in the 1940s had now grown up and wanted to embrace a stage family that remained together despite the odds. Whatever the reasons, *The Sound of Music* was the longest running American musical in West End history, until it was surpassed by *Chicago* five decades later.

By the time the Broadway version closed in 1964, it had run 1,443 performances, with Mary Martin playing the lead in nearly half of them. The touring company with Florence Henderson performed in thirty-five American cities, canceling its run early, sadly enough, on the day after

President Kennedy died, November 23, 1963. A successful production opened in Melbourne, Australia, in October 1961, starring the glorious soprano June Bronhill, and another opened in South Africa in 1963.

Impressive as they were, these triumphs paled next to a brief article in June 1960 in the showbiz bible, *Variety*. *The Sound of Music* had been sold to 20th Century Fox for the record sum of $1,250,000. Had the Broadway production, which eventually cost $480,000, not already recouped most of that at the box office, the sale of the movie rights would have instantly put the show in the black. Rodgers and Hammerstein, in their dual capacities as co-creators and producers, made almost $700,000 between them from the sale. Among other perks negotiated by the fabled Irving "Swifty" Lazar, agent for the creative team behind *The Sound of Music*, was a 10 percent share of any motion picture gross in excess of $12,500,000. That negotiation point seemed a waste of time to Howard Lindsay—what picture ever made more than that? Still, Rodgers and

LEFT: Jean Bayless leads the London company of The Sound of Music in "Do Re Mi." The West End version would run years longer than its Broadway counterpart.

ABOVE: While Maria von Trapp was entertaining little children on Broadway, Elaine Stritch was being tormented by them in Noel Coward's shipboard musical, Sail Away, in 1961.

Hammerstein's vehicles did very well at the box office and 20th Century Fox had successfully produced most of the movie versions, winning a slew of Academy Awards in different categories, including five for *The King and I* in 1956. Any immediate expectations were moot, anyway; contractually the movie could not be released until the end of 1964, to ensure the maximum potential run on stage.

The influence of *The Sound of Music* was starting to be heard in the sound of American music. The original cast album enjoyed a tremendous success. Recorded by Columbia Records the Sunday after the opening, the album was ranked number one for 16 weeks and remained on the charts for 276 weeks—nearly long enough to share the charts with the movie soundtrack album, which itself stayed on the charts for 233 weeks. The original cast album ranks with *My Fair Lady* and the soundtrack album to *West Side Story* as one of the most enduring recordings of Broadway material ever made. The combined sales of the Broadway and movie recordings of *The Sound of Music* make it the most popular musical score of all time.

Success of any kind brings with it both tribute and mockery and, in 1961, Noel Coward set his expert hand to the latter in his brand-new Broadway show, *Sail Away*. Although both Rodgers and Mary Martin were fond colleagues of Coward's, the witty playwright-songwriter-actor—who could be quite sentimental himself, given the occasion—had very little tolerance for children, on or off stage. Supposedly, during a very long West End musical with a particularly egregious kiddie actor at the center of it, Coward remarked, "Two things should be cut—the second act and that child's throat." He had his chance to get back at all stage moppets—von Trapps, included—in Act Two of *Sail Away*. The perfect instrument of his revenge was the tart and cynical star Elaine Stritch, a kind of anti–Mary Martin. Playing the beleaguered entertainment director of a transatlantic cruise, Stritch had, at one point in the show, to entertain a score of raucous kiddies in the ship's playroom. To get them to be quiet she teaches them "The Little Ones' A.B.C.":

MIMI:
Try, if it's possible to keep on key,
Sing the letters after me.

CHILDREN:
Just how corny can you be?

MIMI:
If you sing when you are blue
You find you
Never have to care a rap,
When the skies are dark and grey,
You just say—

CHILDREN:
What a load of crap!

Even without a movie version of *The Sound of Music*, audiences across the country were familiar enough with the show by 1962 to laugh at a more direct parody. In June of that year, CBS televised a live concert featuring both Broadway's reigning leading lady and its most recently celebrated comedienne. "Julie and Carol at Carnegie Hall" was a supreme showcase for the singing, dancing, and comic talents of Julie Andrews and Carol Burnett. Although neither woman had yet starred in a feature film or a television series, the Carnegie Hall audience (and their living-room counterparts) ate up Julie and Carol's antics, which included many duets and several parodies. One of these featured Julie and Carol in Tyrolean peasant frocks and aprons, accompanied by what look like several dozen chorus boys in lederhosen and Peter Pan hats. Andrews stepped forward and announced, "We are the happy Swiss Family Pratt. We sing you a happy song that I used to sing when I was a happy nun back in Switzerland." As far as Julie Andrews knew at the time, she was simply making fun of the smash-hit musical that was running concurrently with her stint as Guinevere in *Camelot*. Walt Disney came to see a matinee performance of *Camelot* and immediately thought of Andrews playing the magical nanny in his next movie, *Mary Poppins*. During rehearsals of the television concert, Andrews asked Burnett if she thought the Disney movie was a good idea. Clearly she thought it couldn't hurt, and soon Andrews was off to Hollywood to make her first feature film.

However, by the time Andrews was in front of the cameras, Hollywood seemed to have forgotten completely about *The Sound of Music*. 20th Century Fox had left its $1.25 million investment sitting in a file cabinet on the studio lot in Culver City. In 1962, a major box-office smash would have meant the difference between life and death for Fox Studios. Fox was in a precarious financial situation, having installed some less-than-savvy executives who had sunk millions of dollars into the epic movie biography *Cleopatra*, starring Elizabeth Taylor and Richard Burton. As millions of good dollars were being thrown after bad at the Cinecetta Studios in Rome, where *Cleopatra* was shooting, Fox founder and producer Darryl Zanuck returned to Hollywood with a plan to seize control of the studio, which was on the brink of bankruptcy. The Fox board was thrilled to give the reins back to Zanuck, and he installed his son, Richard, to take over as vice president of production in California.

Faced with minimal funds, Richard Zanuck pared Fox down to a skeletal staff that roamed the vast studio back lot like it was a graveyard. Resources had to be marshaled to put something into production and Zanuck scoured the studio's script library to find a potential block-buster. It had been sitting there all along. "I thought *The Sound of Music* was such a wonderful piece of family entertainment," recounted Zanuck to Julia Antopol Hirsch for her comprehensive *The Sound of Music: The Making of America's Favorite Movie*. "And it had been so hugely successful, it was just an obvious thing to do. Even though the studio couldn't release the picture until the play

"EVEN THOUGH THE STUDIO COULDN'T RELEASE THE PICTURE UNTIL THE PLAY CLOSED, THEY COULD HAVE PUT A WRITER ON IT. WHAT YOU WANT TO DO IS HAVE YOUR MOVIE READY FOR RELEASE WHEN YOUR DATE COMES." RICHARD ZANUCK

ABOVE: When in Rome: Despite Noel Coward's parody of Rodgers' work, they continued to be close chums, building on their friendship from the late 1920s. Here Rodgers pays a visit to the set of Androcles and the Lion, a 1967 television musical for which he composed both music and lyrics. Coward, always in charge, played Caesar.

closed, they could have put a writer on it. What you want to do is have your movie ready for release when your date comes."

It was obvious which writer Zanuck would put on the project. Ernest Lehman was one of Hollywood's most successful screenwriters; he had scripted Hitchcock's *North by Northwest*, as well as adapting acclaimed screen versions of the Broadway musicals *West Side Story* and Rodgers and Hammerstein's *The King and I*. Besides his impeccable reputation as an adaptor of remarkable fidelity to the original material, Lehman also thought *The Sound of Music* had huge potential to be a movie success. He and his wife had seen it on Broadway a few weeks after it opened and, during intermission, it occurred to Lehman that, despite the drubbing that the musical had taken from the New York intelligentsia, it might work even better on screen. Lehman was as sharp as they come— based on his own hardscrabble experience as a Broadway press agent, he wrote (with Clifford Odets) one of the most cynical movies of all time, *Sweet Smell of Success*— and if he could open up his heart to a cinematic *The Sound of Music*, maybe audiences could as well.

After Lehman was officially signed in December 1962, he and Zanuck moved forward to put the pieces of the production together. During their first lunch date to discuss the assignment, Zanuck was approached by Swifty Lazar, who offered to buy the property back for $2 million. Rumor had it that Jack Warner, the head of Warner Bros, wanted to keep *The Sound of Music* off the market so it would not compete with his upcoming multimillion-dollar *My Fair Lady*. Zanuck refused the $750,000 windfall. (Fiscal instability must have been on many people's minds at the Fox studio; when Burt Lancaster encountered Lehman at the Fox commissary a few weeks after the screenwriter had signed his contract for *The Sound of Music*, Lancaster reportedly snarled at him, "Jesus, you must need the money!") Zanuck and Lehman now concentrated on directors. Their first choice was Robert Wise, a much-respected director who started as an editor and, early in his career, edited *Citizen Kane*. Wise had just won an Academy Award as Best Director for *West Side Story* (with codirector Jerome Robbins); Lehman had enjoyed his collaboration with Wise on that picture, but Wise was busy preparing a huge blockbuster for Fox already, a naval epic called *The Sand Pebbles*.

Zanuck and Lehman went down the list of successful directors of movie musicals and were rejected by both Stanley Donen and Gene Kelly. Then, Zanuck's father, Darryl, suggested William Wyler. Although Wyler had never directed a musical before, he was a titan of Hollywood's golden age, having helmed such classics as *The Little Foxes*, *The Best Years of Our Lives*, and *Ben-Hur*. He was also a German émigré, having arrived in Hollywood in the 1920s, and paid his dues working on Westerns. Lehman thought it an inspired idea and took Wyler to see the show on Broadway, which proved not to be such a great idea—Wyler hated it. But he kept asking Lehman to talk him into the project, so in May 1963, armed with an outline of the script, Wyler, Lehman, and Roger Edens, a highly regarded musical supervisor and arranger during the glory days of the MGM musical, flew to Salzburg to scout locations that could bring the project to life. The trip would later prove to

ABOVE: *Screenwriter Ernest Lehman had written some of the most hard-boiled screenplays in town; still, he thought there might be a terrific movie in* The Sound of Music. *Here he is, scouting locations in Salzburg.*

RIGHT: *Director Robert Wise had made his initial reputation as a film editor—one can practically see him cutting the movie together in his head as he helms the early Hollywood shoot of* The Sound of Music. *Sadly, Lehman and Wise, the two men who contributed so much to the success of the movie, died within three months of each other in 2005.*

be a profitable one for the eventual look and success of the movie, but when they returned in September and Lehman submitted a first draft to Wyler, Fox was no closer to sealing the deal with the director. Suddenly, books on martial history appeared on Wyler's desk, and Zanuck and Lehman were concerned that Wyler had become preoccupied with the events of the *Anschluss*. It became clear that, for Wyler, the historical events were more persuasive than the musical ones in *The Sound of Music*. Zanuck and Lehman's concerns were rendered moot by the fall of 1963; Wyler took another movie, *The Collector*, and left the partners holding the bag of a multimillion-dollar movie without a director.

As luck or chance would have it, Robert Wise's picture for Fox, *The Sand Pebbles*, was experiencing production difficulties and had been postponed. Lehman used this opportunity to unofficially slip a draft of *The Sound of Music* to Wise. Wise, to his surprise, was impressed by what Lehman had done and started listening to the cast album of the Broadway show. He sought advice from a friend and colleague, Saul Chaplin, whose musical acumen on movie projects was second to none. Chaplin, who had worked as associate producer on the movie of *West Side Story*, had not loved the Broadway version of *The Sound of Music* but he loved what Lehman had done with it, so he encouraged Wise to go ahead. The director signed his contract in November 1963. With the hopes of getting cameras rolling by spring 1964, Wise and Chaplin took a jaunt to Salzburg to scout locations.

With Wise signed, the new creative team had to think seriously about casting. Mary Martin, who had not made a movie in nearly twenty years, was clearly not an option to play Maria. Doris Day, then at the height of her box-office power, was being pitched heavily by her agent. Other names considered were Leslie Caron, Anne Bancroft, and Shirley Jones, but the name of Julie Andrews kept cropping up. Andrews had been notoriously passed over for the chance to reprise her famous role as Eliza Doolittle in the movie of *My Fair Lady*, in favor of Audrey Hepburn. Still, by early 1964, she already had two movies in the can awaiting release—*Mary Poppins* and *The Americanization of Emily*, initially slated to be directed by William Wyler. Robert Wise recounted the talent search in a 2005 documentary:

> I knew about Julie. I heard about her. I'd never met her, never seen her. There was a certain rumor around town that she might not be as photogenic as she ideally could be. Well, this gave us pause. So we got an okay to call the producer of *Mary Poppins*, asked if we could come over and see some of the cut film to see how she was. So I went over there with Ernie Lehman and Saul Chaplin to see it. And we saw two or three minutes of it, and the minute she came on, that was it, no question. We went right back to the studio and said, "That's our girl. Sign her."

Soon after contract negotiations began with Julie Andrews, Wise, Lehman, and Chaplin visited Richard Rodgers in New York. Rodgers was so averse to having his properties tampered with by Hollywood that he and Hammerstein had produced the movie version of *Oklahoma!* themselves. It still did very little to mollify his unease about the movies, but as the only living member of the Rodgers and Hammerstein team, not only was his permission required to make certain changes, but his creative advice would be invaluable. Rodgers was very open to writing two new songs for the movie—in the years since Hammerstein's death, he had tried his hand at crafting lyrics as well as music—and the movie team was thrilled by his enthusiasm and collaboration. Then, the conversation steered round to casting the part of Maria von Trapp.

Rodgers, who could be as cynical as anyone, looked at Lehman and snorted, "I suppose you're going to cast Doris Day, huh?"

*ABOVE: The King and Us. Robert Wise (center) and his associate
producer Saul Chaplin (right) pay a crucial visit to Richard Rodgers
in New York.*

MY FAVORITE THINGS

Raindrops on roses and whiskers on kittens,
Bright copper kettles and warm woolen mittens,
Brown paper packages tied up with strings—
These are a few of my favorite things.

Cream-colored ponies and crisp apple strudels,
Doorbells and sleigh-bells and schnitzel with noodles,
Wild geese that fly with the moon on their wings—
These are a few of my favorite things.

Girls in white dresses with blue satin sashes,
Snowflakes that stay on my nose and eyelashes,
Silver-white winters that melt into springs—
These are a few of my favorite things.

When the dog bites,
When the bee stings,
When I'm feeling sad,
I simply remember my favorite things
And then I don't feel so bad!

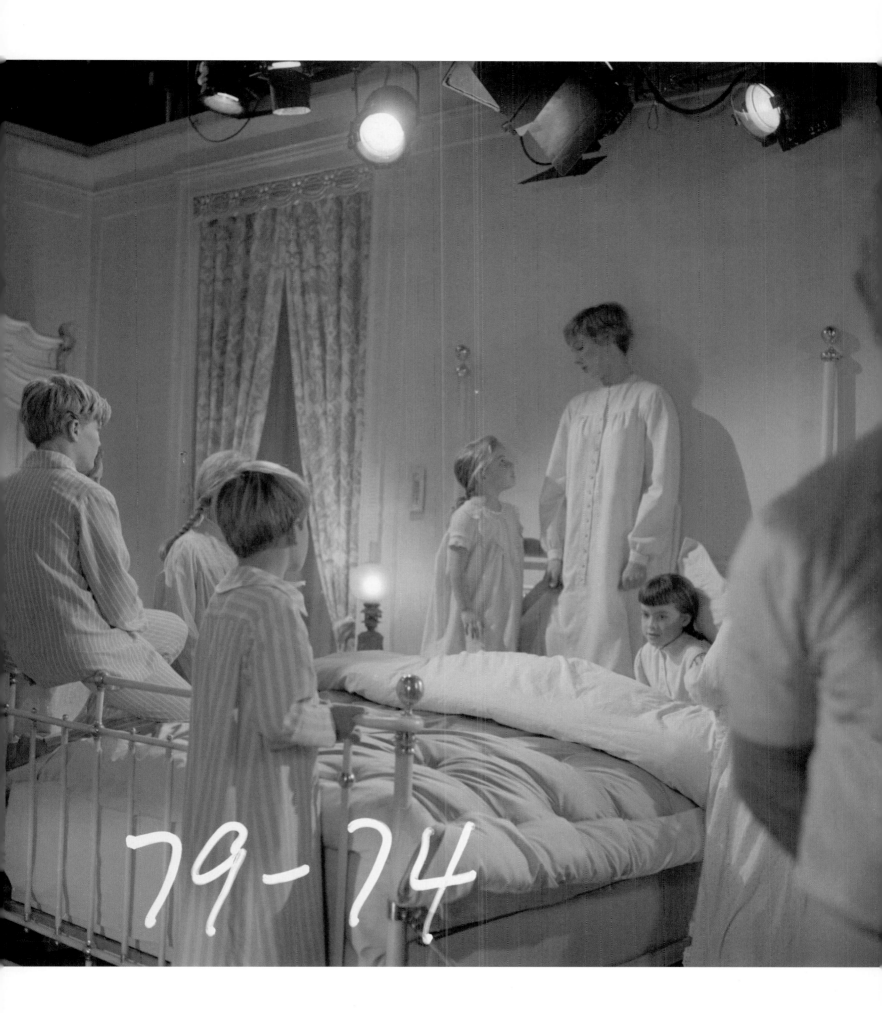

79-74

"Happy Song" is not much of a title, but in Oscar Hammerstein's early outline for the show, he clearly intended for Maria to sing something upbeat in the middle of Act One. Audiences who know "My Favorite Things" only from the movie version would be very surprised at how this quintessentially upbeat number appears in the Broadway show. Before Maria ventures forth to the von Trapp villa for the first time, she and the Mother Abbess bond by sharing a song about their favorite things from their respective childhoods, so, originally, there was nary a von Trapp child in sight during the entire number. (And no Salzburger worth his *salz* would ever think fondly of schnitzel with noodles—the dish does not exist in Austria.)

Nearly a year after the show opened, the sound of a different kind of music was recorded. John Coltrane was the major avant-garde saxophonist of his time, but as the 1960s dawned, he was actually experimenting with a return to melody. Coltrane went into the Atlantic Records studio to lay down some tunes for a new album. For his first cut, he chose Rodgers' lilting waltz, "My Favorite Things." With his sidemen McCoy Tyner, Elvin Jones, and Steve Davis, he doubled the time to 6/8 and turned the tune into an extended fourteen-minute riff, weaving in exotic East Indian phrasings and transforming it into a jazz standard. At once respectful and iconoclastic, Coltrane brought the sheer pleasure of Rodgers' musical architecture to thousands of listeners who would not be caught dead inside the Lunt-Fontanne Theater.

In the movie version, screenwriter Ernest Lehman made a simple and brilliant "swap" between "My Favorite Things" and "The Lonely Goatherd." In the stage version, Maria sings "The Lonely Goatherd" on her first night at the villa in order to cheer up the children during a thunderstorm. According to Julie Andrews, in the 2005 documentary "My Favorite Things":

> Ernie thought that it would be so much better, from the point of view of the lyrics and everything else, to use "My Favorite Things." What better way to cheer children up than to take their mind off the storm outside and to talk about all the things that you love and that make you feel cozy and comfy? I think it was an inspired decision.

To director Robert Wise's great pleasure, Lehman, who obviously had to craft some original dialogue for a completely different setting, made the transition into the song effortless: "Ernie rewrote the dialogue leading into the songs in almost every instance so you could just slide into it. It was very effective and very important." In fact, Andrews simply speaks the first few lines of the lyrics.

For such a key number in terms of the movie's development of character, it is somewhat surprising that "My Favorite Things" was shot on only the second day of filming. Andrews had to work overtime to create the necessary rapport with the children, but if anyone could build a relationship with seven young actors quickly, it was Julie Andrews. "She put the kids at ease and made them easy to work with," recounted Wise. "She even taught them to sing 'Supercalifragilisticexpialidocious.'" And that was half a year before *Mary Poppins* was released by the Walt Disney Studios, thereby adding yet another item to the long list of favorite things people admire about Julie Andrews.

PAGE 95: Amazingly, this key number in the movie was filmed on the second day of shooting.

RIGHT: Oscar Hammerstein's initial list of "favorite things."

FAR RIGHT: Like a star who is learning to pray: Robert Wise gives his leading lady some religious instruction.

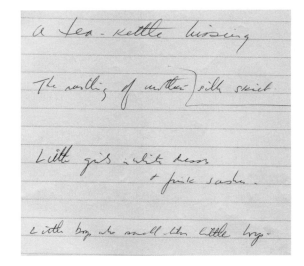

79-307

CHAPTER FIVE

HOLLYWOOD TO SALZBURG

When Julie Andrews gave her first audition for Richard Rodgers in 1955, she was just like Mary Martin in 1938—a bright, pert, engaging young singer and the toast of Broadway, thanks to the import of a British spoof of 1920s musicals called *The Boy Friend*, which had opened the season before. Rodgers and Hammerstein were casting a rather different kind of musical, *Pipe Dream*, set among the hard-luck heroes and riff-raff of John Steinbeck's *Cannery Row*. Andrews auditioned for the role of Suzy, a prostitute in Steinbeck's original stories, but here she was more of a hard-bitten dreamer, drifting through the louche Monterrey scene. Although the thoroughly charming Andrews was born in England, Rodgers and Hammerstein, who had frequently gambled on new talent, were eager to see what she could do.

As Rodgers sat in the middle of that "big black giant"—Hammerstein's phrase for the theater—Andrews belted out a semi-operatic song. As she recounted on the Thirteen/American Masters documentary on Rodgers, *The Sweetest Sounds*:

> I gave it my all. And he came up onstage afterwards and he looked at me and he said, "that was absolutely . . . adequate" and I went "Oh!" Then he said, "No, no I'm just teasing you. It was lovely."

Rodgers asked her if she were auditioning for anything else, and she admitted she had been auditioning for the long-awaited musical adaptation of George Bernard Shaw's *Pygmalion* by Alan Jay Lerner and Frederick Loewe.

> And he looked at me for a very long time, and then he said, "Oh. I tell you what. If they ask you to do that show, I think you should. But if you don't do that show, I wish you would let us know because we would very much like to use you."

It was not only, as Andrews admitted, generous advice, but also a close shave. *Pipe Dream*, which opened in November 1955, was Rodgers and Hammerstein's only real commercial flop. *My Fair Lady*, the musical treatment of Shaw, opened four months later, starring Andrews. It was, in its time, the greatest success the Broadway musical had ever brought forth into the world, and it made Andrews, in the words of Richard Rodgers, "Broadway's most radiant new star—there wasn't a composer or lyricist who didn't start dreaming of songs for her to sing or roles for her to play."

When the original television special *Cinderella* was broadcast on March 31, 1957, it was watched by 107 million people in the United States—more people than there were television sets. Rodgers and Hammerstein wrote a charming score, full of sentiment without being sentimental, and Julie Andrews had the opportunity to share the soundstage with playwright Howard Lindsay, who, in one of his forays into the acting world, played the befuddled King. The show introduced Andrews to a far wider audience than had admired her on the Great White Way.

Six years later, when Robert Wise went to Julie Andrews with the offer to star as Maria von Trapp, she had not yet appeared in a feature film. The opportunity presented by *The Sound of Music* was a huge one, but Andrews was not immediately sure she wanted to be in another musical. *Mary Poppins* had yet to be released and she was enjoying filming the straight dramatic lead in *The Americanization of Emily*. Andrews had another concern, as well: she thought the original material might be too saccharine to play well on the big screen. However, once she agreed to take the part (according to Julia Hirsch's history of the movie, Fox eventually offered her $225,000 for a two-picture deal), she sat down with Wise at the Fox studio restaurant and expressed her reservations. He explained to her that he wanted to take a less sentimental, more textured approach to the material. Apparently, a spoonful of medicine helped the sugar go down and Andrews was both appeased and inspired to begin her work with Wise, whom she later credited for giving her a master class in movie-acting technique.

With Andrews signed (Wise and Saul Chaplin first discovered the news in Louella Parsons' gossip column while they were scouting locations in Salzburg), the attention turned to casting Captain von Trapp. Fox executives were keen on Bing Crosby, but Wise never took that suggestion seriously. William Wyler, during the time he was considering directing the picture, courted Rex Harrison. (Although the thought of a *My Fair Lady* reunion with Julie Andrews is a provocative one, Harrison would have been badly miscast.)

Other names submitted to Wise included Sean Connery, Peter Finch, Louis Jourdan, and Maximillian Schell. Yul Brynner lobbied extensively for the part. The notion of having Brynner reprise a stern patriarch in a Rodgers and Hammerstein score might have seemed like a sure thing at the box office, but Wise was determined not to weigh down *The Sound of Music* with more clichés than it could already handle. He had been impressed with a classical actor who, while only thirty-five years old, had taken the stages of London, New York, and his native Canada by storm: Christopher Plummer.

Plummer had extensive experience performing onstage and in serious drama on television, but his movie career, in 1963, was nothing to write home about. Still, he was lukewarm to Wise's advances; for an actor who had played Hamlet, Mercutio, and Cyrano de Bergerac, Georg von Trapp seemed to Plummer stiff and dull—in his own words, "a frightful square." Scriptwriter Ernest Lehman was sent to convince Plummer, and together they collaborated on drawing out some of the Captain's (and Plummer's) ironical sense of humor, adding a pervading sadness that gave the character some additional depth. Lehman was thrilled to have Plummer's suggestions and it was Lehman's enthusiasm that convinced Plummer to sign on the dotted line.

Wise now had two youthful, attractive, talented leads who were largely unknown as international movie stars, so he filled the rest of the adult roles with a mixture of familiar faces. Richard Haydn, a beloved character actor from the 1940s, took on the role of the self-serving impresario Max Detweiler (although it is intriguing to imagine what one of Wise's suggestions—Noel Coward—would have done with the part). The stylish and elegant Hollywood star Eleanor Parker was cast as Baroness Elsa Schraeder. Parker, also a Hollywood fixture since the early 1940s, was probably the most well-known cast member prior to the movie's release.

For the children, Wise and his casting consultants interviewed hundreds of young actors and actresses in London, New York, and Los Angeles before asking nearly 200 of them to audition for him. Casting one child actor is difficult enough; casting seven who must be credible as a family—in addition to being personable, musical, and the right height—is a huge challenge. Unlike the previous stage incarnations, Wise decided the von Trapp children should not all be blond and Aryan-looking, but have a physical and emotional variety among them. He whittled the number of actors down to fourteen—two families of seven each—mixed and matched them, and finally chose his seven children in time to begin rehearsal on February 10, 1964.

Well, six children. The part of Liesl was proving difficult to cast. She had to appear to be a naïve sixteen

PAGE 98: *Richard Rodgers helps Julie Andrews prepare for her television debut as Cinderella, 1957.*

PAGES 100–101: *Not Salzburg, but a magical re-creation: the Fox lot provided the landscape for the von Trapp villa. One can glimpse the gazebo—re-created from the one left behind at the Salzburg location.*

ABOVE: *Do they love her because she's beautiful? Or talented? Or charming? Oscar Hammerstein and Richard Rodgers pay a visit to Andrews during the photo call for Cinderella. Sadly, Hammerstein would never get to see Andrews play the lead in The Sound of Music.*

ABOVE: "Willowy" describes the background, the dress, and the essence of Julie Andrews in this studio portrait taken in Salzburg. The Sound of Music would establish her reputation as one of the 1960s' leading film actresses.

RIGHT: Christopher Plummer, along with such greats as John Barrymore (whom he portrayed in a one-man Broadway show) and Laurence Olivier, was one of the few great classical actors who could also make the transition into a dashing film matinee idol.

(going on seventeen, of course) and still be engaging enough to hold down the romantic subplot. Wise auditioned such future stars as Mia Farrow, Victoria Tennant, Lesley Ann Warren, and Teri Garr, but Wise and the casting people kept coming back to Charmian Farnon, a poised and fetching young woman who had no previous acting, singing, or dancing experience. Farnon was signed nearly two weeks after the other children were already in rehearsal on the Fox lot. There were two slight problems: Farnon was actually twenty-one, going on twenty-two, and her last name simply would not do. The latter issue was resolved with a name change to Charmian Carr and the former would have to be settled by costumes and lighting—

Carr certainly would not be the first movie ingénue not to act her age.

A product of the Hollywood system for the previous twenty-five years, Wise had nothing but respect for the craftspeople in the industry and he staffed his movie with some of the best. The director of photography, Ted McCord, had a career that started in the 1920s. He had cut his teeth shooting hundreds of Westerns in the 1930s and 1940s—his mastery of outdoor locations would come in handy—and he had just worked for Wise on *Two for the Seesaw*. So had Russian-born production designer Boris Leven, who had coordinated the complicated interior/exterior designs for Wise's *West Side Story* and was rewarded with an Academy

Award for his work. Costume designer Dorothy Jeakins knew how to put together a complicated epic: she worked for Cecil B. DeMille on several movies and designed the movie version of Rodgers and Hammerstein's *South Pacific*. Jeakins' work on *The Sound of Music* was both bold and subtle. Her playclothes for the children, pasted together from heavy curtains with gold satin sashes, were unforgettable and the transition in Andrews' costumes from youthfully awkward to a solid maturity demonstrated a brilliant grasp of character. That might be why Wise rewarded her with a cameo in the movie—she plays a nun in the opening sequence.

Producer/director Wise also surrounded himself with the two gentlemen who had done so much to make *West*

LEFT: The von Trapp children, cinematic version (from left)

● **Kym Karath (Gretl)** was five years old when filming started and impressed Robert Wise immediately with her confidence. She now divides her time between the East and West Coasts of the United States, and has returned to acting.

● **Debbie Turner (Marta)** was seven when filming began. She currently lives in the Midwestern United States, where she has a career as a floral designer.

● **Angela Cartwright (Brigitta** – or Louisa, if you're being fooled) was eleven and had already enjoyed a successful television sitcom career. She now lives in Los Angeles and is an artist/photographer as well as an aspiring producer.

● **Duane Chase (Kurt)** was thirteen years old. He now lives in Seattle, Washington, and works as a software engineer.

● **Heather Menzies (the real Louisa)** was fourteen, playing a thirteen-year-old. She made a few more feature films in her twenties, but now works for a cancer foundation in Los Angeles, established in honor of her late husband, TV star Robert Urich.

● **Nicholas Hammond (Friedrich)** was thirteen when filming began, and remembered seeing Julie Andrews on stage in the London production of My Fair Lady in the late 1950s. He went on to do some television work (he was the first live-action Spider-Man on American TV), but has since moved to Australia, where he works as a screenwriter.

● **Charmian Carr (Liesl)** was actually twenty-one going on twenty-two when she was cast in the film, without any prior acting experience. She has continued her relationship with the movie to this day, serving as hostess for numerous performances of Singalong Sound of Music across America, and as the author of two related books: her best-selling memoir, Forever Liesl, and its sequel, Letters to Liesl. She now resides outside of Los Angeles, where she has a thriving practice as an interior designer.

We all know that Julie Andrews and Christopher Plummer went on to international stardom ..

ABOVE: *And I'll sing once more: Under the baton of Irwin Kostal, Julie Andrews does another prerecording take for her friend and mentor, associate producer Saul Chaplin.*

RIGHT: COWABUNGA! *Nicholas Hammond and Duane Chase take the California surfing craze of the 1960s to the Fox lot.*

Side Story a resounding, award-winning success: associate producer Saul Chaplin and screenwriter Ernest Lehman. Chaplin, a musical jack of all trades, was instrumental in envisioning the musical numbers for the screen, especially for the Salzburg locations. Lehman's contributions were inestimable. Not only did he do an inspired job of restructuring the musical numbers so that they serve the needs of cinematic narrative, he skillfully took the best of Lindsay and Crouse's book and supplemented it with his own dialogue and invention in a seamless way.

Surely Lehman's greatest contribution is the way he opened up the stage version for the movies. "Opening up" is a slightly misunderstood phrase—it is not just substituting an outdoor location for an interior one. All one has to do is watch the movie version of *My Fair Lady* to see how earthbound a movie musical can be. Although *My Fair Lady* makes extensive use of the Warner Bros. backlot, it feels suffocatingly claustrophobic; there does not appear to be an inch of real blue sky. Once Lehman realized how important Salzburg would be to the texture of the movie, he did an exemplary job of marrying the exterior locations to the narrative. Robert Wise and his crew realized Lehman's vision in a masterful way; rather than reproduce the clichés of a movie musical, Wise and company made a first-class movie that just happened to be a musical.

First, though, were the rehearsals for the principals at the Fox lot in Culver City. They began with the children rehearsing their musical numbers with Chaplin, music supervisor Irwin Kostal (also a *West Side Story* alumnus), and the choreography team of Marc Breaux and Dee Dee Wood. Breaux and Wood had already worked with Andrews on *Mary Poppins* and they had a superb sense of how the cameras could take their work into another dimension. Wood explained to Julia Hirsch, "As opposed to a proscenium on the stage, where you just have a picture that you look at, one picture—boom, boom—audience and the performance, right there. Now, when we're doing a film, we can go all over the place." (But there was room for improvement—when Lehman saw an early run-through of the pillow-throwing segment of "My Favorite Things," he thought it was far too meticulously choreographed and suggested that Breaux and Wood create something more spontaneous. They agreed and, by and large, the movie is mercifully devoid of that "hey-look-at-me" quality that mars so many movie adaptations of Broadway material.)

In March, the complex process of prerecording began under the baton of Irwin Kostal. By then, both Andrews and Plummer had reported for duty. Prerecording musical numbers with a full orchestra is difficult in any motion picture, but the cast of *The Sound of Music* had to record their songs weeks before filming began (not to mention before filming in a city not one of them had set foot in). Julie Andrews explained the complexity: "You have to try to imagine exactly what you might be doing without knowing in any way what you'll be doing." In other words, if you get to the location shoot and want to chuckle as you skip across a meadow, it must synch up to the playback recorded months before, or you are out of luck. Still, pre-recording went particularly smoothly (Andrews is an acknowledged pro at laying down tracks) and, some issues of dubbing notwithstanding (see the section on "Edelweiss"), cameras began to roll on March 26, 1964.

The first week of initial shooting in Los Angeles began with the storm sequence in Maria's bedroom and included "My Favorite Things" (revised pillow fight included). Next, most of the Nonnberg Abbey interior sequences were filmed. (From their location scouting the previous November, Wise and his crew knew that the nuns at the actual Nonnberg would not let them film interiors there.) Boris Leven had done such an impressive job re-creating the cloister and graveyard that, for years, tour guides in Salzburg thought the graveyard was a location site near St. Peter's Church. By April 17, initial filming was completed and they would shoot the remaining interiors—the von Trapp villa, the outdoor pavilion, etc.—during the summer.

Finally it was time for the cast and crew to be introduced to their co-star. She had been around for many years, acquiring an intimidating reputation for beauty and charm. No matter how talented the cast was, the movie of *The Sound of Music* would never come alive unless the actors knew how to handle this majestic leading lady. She could make or break the movie.

It was time to face Salzburg.

THE LONELY GOATHERD

During Maria's first night at the villa, each of the children sneaks into her room for comfort during a thunderstorm. In order to cheer them up, she sings "The Lonely Goatherd."

Moviegoers may be slightly confused at this description. In the movie, Maria sings "My Favorite Things." However, as one can clearly see in Oscar Hammerstein's original draft of the lyrics for that scene, the song that was supposed to be used was "The Lonely Goatherd" (which began life as the "Yodel Song"— a musical set in the Austrian Alps had to have some yodeling). The song was closely integrated into the action of the scene and his dramatic instincts were on obvious display in the way he crafted the assignment of the singing parts in the original number.

Though Hammerstein usually eschewed all the fancy or clever lyrics mastered by such peers as Cole Porter or Rodgers' first partner, Lorenz Hart, here he really pushes the envelope when rhyming "goatherd":

—Men on a road with a load to tote, heard
—Men in the midst of a table d'hôte, heard
—Men drinking beer with the foam afloat, heard

When the filmmakers reconceived (and reset) the song, they were inspired by the famous Salzburg Marionettes to turn the number into a puppet show. The actual Marionette troupe refused the offer to participate, so Robert Wise turned to Bil Baird's Marionettes, an American puppetry ensemble. Bil (and his wife, Cora) had been enchanting stage, movie, and TV audiences with their puppetry for decades when Wise contracted them for their most famous assignment.

How the film's impresario, Max Detweiler, gets inspired by a puppet show to produce a vocal concert at the Salzburg Festival is another story (and leap of faith) entirely.

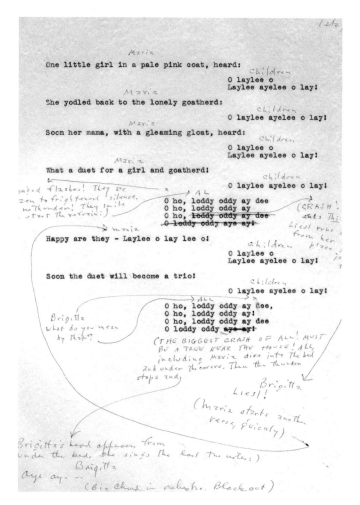

PAGES 110–111 Robert Wise sets up the shots for "The Lonely Goatherd."

FAR LEFT: The Bil Baird puppeteers are actually pulling the strings in this shot.

TOP LEFT: Hammerstein's notations to the song lyrics provide a full scenario—he always thought as a dramatist first.

TOP RIGHT: Choreographer Dee Dee Wood's notes for the sequence.

LEFT: Is our lonely goatherd pitching Robert Wise a new version of Pinocchio?

CHAPTER SIX
SALZBURG AND BEYOND

Wolfgang Amadeus Mozart was Salzburg's number one pop star for 200 years, until the city's favorite son was knocked off the charts by two native-born New Yorkers, Rodgers and Hammerstein.

Mozart is Salzburg's most celebrated progeny and prodigy. Born in 1756, on the Getreidegasse, in the middle of the city, Mozart considered Salzburg his home city during his tragically brief life. His father was the city's leading musician and concertmaster, but once he saw his son's precocious musical gifts, he took young Wolfgang on a tour to perform before the crowned heads of Europe. Mozart settled back in Salzburg briefly in 1774 before seeking his fame and fortune in Italy, Prague, and Vienna, but he wrote nearly 350 works in his birthplace and premiered several important pieces there. Salzburg has rewarded Mozart with memorials, statues, and museums; his childhood home is a major tourist attraction, his name adorns everything from chocolates to cafés to bridges. And, of course, with the convocation of the Salzburg Festival in 1920, the entire city was alive with the sound of his music.

Salzburg had always been one of Europe's most magical cities. Founded 1,300 years ago, it has retained its magisterial appearance with its medieval fortresses, church spires, and baroque palaces perched on two hills separated by the Salzach River. For centuries, it was an autonomous church state, ruled by powerful and imperious archbishops and, not coincidentally, an independent spirit is an integral part of the Salzburg character. The musical genius of Wolfgang Amadeus Mozart put a human face on Salzburg's exalted majesty and the tradition of his music is one that native Salzburgers hold close to their hearts. Had those good citizens known the different kind of fame about to descend on them when Robert Wise and company set up camp with a small army of cast and crew in April 1964, would they have reacted with something other than a mild indifference?

It was always Wise's intention—and the intention of the studio heads at Fox—to spend no more than six weeks on the Salzburg locations. Location shooting is always expensive, but in the case of *The Sound of Music*, every major cast member who appeared in the Los Angeles interiors also needed to be filmed at the Salzburg exteriors, so the cost of travel, lodging, and catering would be enormous. In addition, Salzburg was not exactly the movie capital of the world, so a supplementary crew with additional equipment had to be brought in from Munich and small studios had to be set up for cover photography in the case of inclement weather.

In the dictionary, under the phrase "inclement weather," there should be a photograph of Salzburg. It has the world's seventh highest annual rainfall, perhaps a trivial detail, but one that had escaped Robert Wise's usually precise attention. Rain was by far the most problematic obstacle faced by the crew; the company's six-week sojourn was stretched to eleven frustrating weeks because of the weather, and what few interior scenes could be covered in local studios were used up quickly. There was a lot of waiting around.

The company seemed to take it all in its stride. Peggy Wood and Anna Lee filmed a good number of their scenes early on, and enjoyed the sightseeing during their days off. They were lodged, along with Christopher Plummer, at the Hotel Bristol, a British-owned hotel that was once the Gestapo headquarters during World War II, and Plummer could be found exercising his musical gifts at the Bristol's piano bar until the wee hours. The Bristol also became the center for hair and makeup every morning. The von Trapp children (and their real mothers and tutors) were in another hotel and Julie Andrews and Robert Wise lodged at a more luxurious hotel (now the elegant Hotel Sacher)—although Andrews, exhausted between each day's shoot and the next day's preparation, barely had any time to enjoy its amenities or Salzburg's charms.

Actual location filming for the wedding scene began at Mondsee Cathedral, a beautiful baroque church rebuilt on a religious site that stretched back to the eighth century, located about a half-hour northwest of Salzburg's city center. Wise had hired about 600 extras, and Dorothy Jeakins outdid herself with Andrews' tulle wedding dress and Plummer's regimental naval uniform. Wise and Ted McCord tracked their camera, perpendicular to the procession, up the nave to the altar with a breathtaking

PAGE 114: The children and Julie Andrews rehearse "Do Re Mi" on the Winkler Terrace, overlooking the Salzach River.

PAGES 116–117: Andrews was not a natural guitar player; associate producer Saul Chaplin badgered her into practicing and practicing between takes. Fortunately—or unfortunately—the Salzburg weather gave her plenty of time between takes.

ABOVE: How often is a mother given away by her daughter? Well, stepdaughter, at any rate. Liesl (Charmian Carr) gives Maria her bridal bouquet in front of the nuns, who finally agree that Maria has solved her own problem.

RIGHT: A beautiful shot of a beautiful shot: Robert Wise's composition for the wedding in Mondsee Cathedral.

ABOVE: During Maria von Trapp's visit to the set, our nonfictional heroine (right) chats with our fictional one (Julie Andrews, left) and Mrs. Robert (Pat) Wise in the Residenzplatz.

RIGHT: Robert Wise (center) is the patient soul of tact, as he waits for the publicity shots to be taken with Maria von Trapp and Christopher Plummer so he can get back to work.

fluidity, as the soundtrack boomed a counterpoint version of "Maria" on a grand cathedral organ. The complicated filming took all of one day. So far, so good.

A week was spent at the next location, the Rock Riding School. Set in the center of Salzburg, it had for centuries been a marble quarry but, in 1693, a local archbishop decided to create a riding academy out of its excavations. Its natural arena made it a perfect venue for the Salzburg Festival two hundred years later, and many concerts and events have been performed there. Although it is unclear if the real von Trapps performed at the Rock Riding School, the cinematic family sang there for the climactic musical sequence in the movie. The sequences went late into the night, with hundreds of extras freezing beneath their summertime costumes; they were certainly not warmed by the sight of uniformed Nazi soldiers patrolling the upper galleries of the arena.

Nonnberg Abbey, such an important part of the actual and fictional story of Maria von Trapp, was off-limits to the filmmakers, but the Mother Superior allowed the crew to shoot some important exteriors. In one sequence, which Ernest Lehman created expressly for the movie, the von Trapp children journey to the Abbey to find out what has happened to Maria. Although there was no actual exterior bell pull outside the gate, the production designer installed one for the shot—the Mother Superior liked the look of it so much, she kept it up there after the shoot, even though it was practically useless.

By the middle of May, three weeks into their shooting schedule, the crew began filming at some of the signature landmarks in the heart of the city—Mirabell Gardens, the Kapitelplatz, the Residenzplatz, and the Domplatz. These would be used for a variety of scenes, mostly the promenades during "Do Re Mi" and Maria's jaunty procession during "I Have Confidence." But, on May 14, Wise and his crew had to face an unexpected challenge: how do you solve a problem like Maria?

The real Maria von Trapp was not lucky enough to have the same relationship with the movie producers that she had with the original Broadway producers. Although Fox was not contractually obligated to pay the von Trapp family any additional money, the studio certainly did not reach out to Maria, either. In her memoirs, she wrote about how difficult it was to get a "producer" on the phone (Wise, one assumes) but, when she finally did, she began telling him how much she wanted the movie's producers to give greater

dimension to the character of her husband, Captain von Trapp. When she launched into her plea, there was a click at the other end of the phone. She had better luck with Ernest Lehman, meeting with him for lunch at New York's St. Regis Hotel in early 1962. Lehman took copious notes and some details, such as Maria's behavior at the Abbey, made it into the movie. (She continued her arguments on behalf of the Captain, which must have influenced Lehman during his discussions with Plummer.) But Robert Wise's position was that the movie was fiction; certainly not a documentary, and not even really a conventional biography. Wise knew from earlier reports—or simply by reading the screenplay—that Maria von Trapp was a force with which to be reckoned and he would be pleased to keep his distance from the "bossy" (his words) Maria von Trapp.

But Maria beat him at his own game. While visiting Italy with her daughter Rosmarie and granddaughter Barbara, Maria heard about the location filming in Salzburg and dropped by unannounced. From a pure publicity point of view, it would have been foolish to turn her away, and Wise was, despite his reservations, a gentleman. He introduced Maria to the cast and crew and gamely offered her a cameo in the background of a location shot in the Residenzplatz as Andrews marches toward the camera during "I Have Confidence." Although even the most eagle-eyed moviegoers would need a telescope to catch a fleeting glimpse of the real Maria, she is there, in her native Austrian dress, crossing the town square. Apparently, she was unaware that movie crews normally shoot

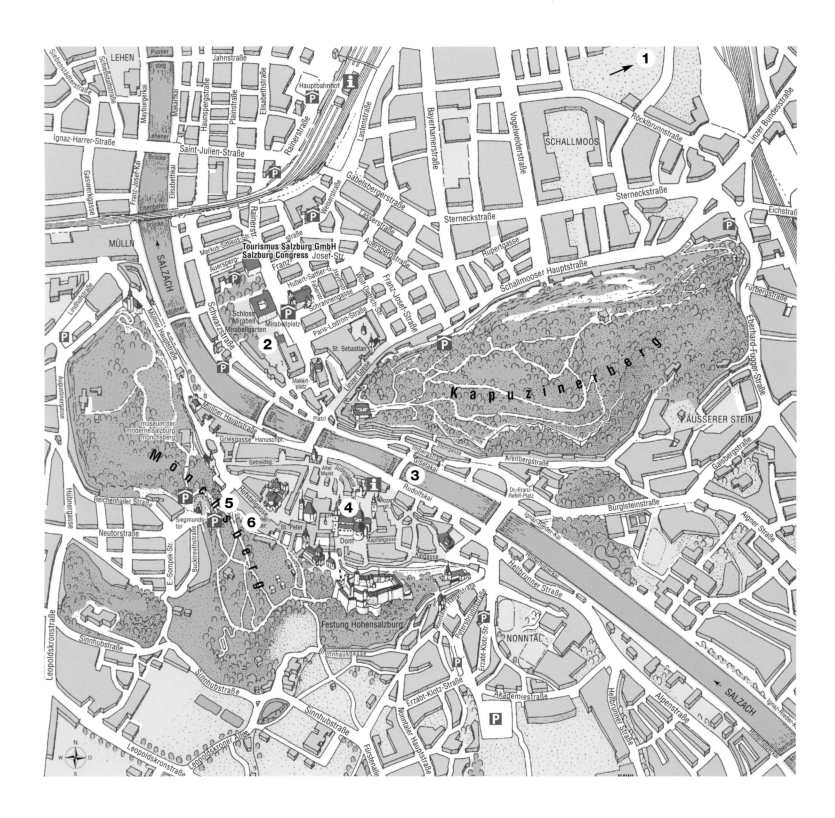

ABOVE AND OPPOSITE: *The sites of Salzburg*

1 Mondsee Cathedral, where the interiors for the wedding were shot.

2 The Mirabell Gardens are part of a stunning Baroque palace and the scene of the "Do Re Mi" climax.

3 The Mozart Footbridge crossing the Salzach River, used in the pre–"Do Re Mi" sequence.

4 The Residenzplatz, a major landmark of the city and site of several key moments.

5 The Horse Pond used in "I Have Confidence."

6 The Rock Riding School, the scene of the movie's final concert and still a musical venue to this day.

1

2

3

4

6

5

ABOVE: *The glamorous Eleanor Parker, as Baroness Schraeder, joins Christopher Plummer on the terrace of Frohnburg Castle.*

RIGHT: *The lakeside view of the von Trapp villa was Leopoldskron Castle, miles away. This is after Maria and the children capsize in front of their father, who is not amused.*

several takes of the same scene and she got quickly bored, even with her two seconds of fame: "That's one ambition I'm giving up," she announced to the press. Wise went quickly—and happily—back to work, while Maria became great chums with Christopher Plummer. She felt that Plummer's dashing incarnation of her husband worked wonders for Georg's reputation. "You are even more handsome than my husband," she cooed to him.

By the end of May, it was time to turn to the extensive number of shots required around the von Trapp villa. The original villa in Aigen had been discounted by location scouts months before, so not one but two separate locations were required to construct the appearance of a grand, elegant lakeside estate. For the façade exteriors, a seventeenth-century castle called Frohnburg was chosen.

The front of Frohnburg was used for the scene where the Captain tears down the Nazi flag, and its courtyard and gates were used for Maria's first appearance at the villa. The rear façade of Frohnburg, with its steps and French windows, was used for several of the scenes among the Captain, Maria, the children, and the Baroness. There was one problem— Frohnburg was not a lakeside estate. Leopoldskron Castle, a five-minute drive away, with its beautiful terrace, handsome stallion-framed balustrade, and lakeside location fit the bill admirably. All of the lakeside scenes shot from the point of view of the villa itself, such as the tumble off the rowing boat into the lake, were filmed at Leopoldskron.

It took nearly a month to capture all the scenes required at the two locations. The Leopoldskron scenes were shot first because rain became a constant nuisance.

Several scenes—Maria's arrival to the villa, a conversation among the Captain, Elsa, and Max—were filmed in the rain, under tarpaulins, with McCord's clever cinematography concealing the precipitation. With the exception of an accident when the boat flipped over and poor Kym Karath (Gretl) nearly drowned, the rain was the only thing that complicated the shooting on Wise's two outdoor sets.

Even the most ardent cineaste must marvel at how well the two locations are cut together within the same sequence. For example, the major confrontation between the Captain and Maria was shot miles and days apart. When the scene begins, Andrews' close-ups are shot at Leopoldskron and Plummer's at Frohnburg:

CAPTAIN: I don't care to hear from you about my children.
MARIA: Well, you must hear from someone. You're not home long enough to know them.
CAPTAIN: I said I don't want to hear—
MARIA: I know you don't—but you've got to. Take Liesl—Liesl isn't a child any more. And if you keep treating her as one, Captain, you're going to have a mutiny on your hands. And Friedrich—Friedrich's afraid to be himself—he's shy—he's aloof, Friedrich needs you—he needs your confidence—
CAPTAIN: Don't tell me about my son . . .

And then later in the scene, after the Captain moves back to the house:

CAPTAIN: Stop! Stop it! You will pack your things and return to the Abbey as soon as you can.
MARIA: I'm sorry. I shouldn't have said those things—not in the way I said them.

The close-ups are reversed: Plummer in front of Frohnburg's rear façade, and Andrews in front of the lake at Leopoldskron. (Astute moviegoers will notice this dialogue is not from Lehman's screenplay, but is taken from Lindsay and Crouse's original libretto. It was a good opportunity to give them credit for writing such an effective scene, though kudos should be given to Lehman for keeping it mostly intact.)

RIGHT: The peak of the Untersberg, courtesy of the Greatest Scenic Designer of Them All, provides a striking background for the picnic that finishes the "My Favorite Things" montage and begins "Do Re Mi."

By the end of June, Wise and his crew had finished all the Trapp villa sequences, but they were several weeks behind schedule. It was now time to go up into the mountains to capture the initial "Do Re Mi" picnic sequences, as well as the "Climb Ev'ry Mountain" finale and the opening shots of "The Sound of Music." If the rain was inconvenient at Frohnburg and Leopoldskron, it was downright perverse in the mountains near Werfen, about thirty miles south of Salzburg. Dreary, bone-chilling rain delayed the shots day after day. The children and Andrews spent most of the time huddled under tarpaulins or in cabins, wrapped in wool blankets to keep warm. According to Andrews' audio commentary for the fortieth anniversary DVD, "Poor Ted McCord, our director of photography, would be out there looking through his little viewfinder at the clouds and giving us a five-minute or three-minute or ten-second warning, and we'd throw off all our warm blankets and get ready for the shot and grab it as quickly as we could."

Once the children's sequences were finished they were sent home (with the exception of Charmian Carr, who stayed on) and the opening shot was tackled. With studio chief Richard Zanuck barking at Wise to shut down location filming and return home immediately, the director knew he had to get Andrews' establishing shot, no matter what. He pleaded with Zanuck to give him one more day, and if he did not get the shot in Austria he would somehow get it in Los Angeles. It was a delirious gamble (where on earth would Wise have gotten that shot in California?), but on that last Thursday, July 2, to paraphrase Ira Gershwin, the clouds broke, and, oh, what a break for the patient Robert Wise.

Wise, Andrews, and the crew packed up their gear and, wanting nothing more than a drop of golden sun, returned to America the next day. The problems with location shooting had added an extra 10 percent to the budget, with a final cost of $9 million. Carr stayed on for a few days to shoot a mini-documentary, *Salzburg: Sights and Sounds*, in which she toured key sites in the city and met up with the Salzburg Marionettes, whose artistry inspired "The Lonely Goatherd." This half-hour movie would be shown for tourism purposes and 20th Century Fox thought it might be useful as a short teaser in movie theaters. Maybe *The Sound of Music* could use the publicity.

DO RE MI

Let's start at the very beginning,
A very good place to start.
When you read you begin with—
A, B, C.
When you sing you begin with do re mi.

Do re mi?

Do re mi.
The first three notes just happen to be
Do re mi.

Doe—a deer, a female deer,
Ray—a drop of golden sun,
Me—a name I call myself,
Far—a long, long way to run,
Sew—a needle pulling thread,
La—a note to follow sew,
Tea—a drink with jam and bread.
That will bring us back to do!

Do re mi fa so la ti do.

MEADOW

23 A

MEADOW
(UP)

C

24

WINKLER
(DOWN)

I f any musical number from the movie has come back to deliver a surprise to audiences of the stage version of *The Sound of Music*, it is "Do Re Mi."

In its theatrical setting, "Do Re Mi" is the first number between Maria and the children; meeting the children in the living room of the von Trapp villa, the new governess teaches them the rudiments of the musical scale. It is a very effective number—even more effective than its precursor from *The King and I*, "Getting to Know You"—and choreographer Joe Layton had worked out a charming bit of business where Mary Martin patted each of the children on the head with a respective note on the scale, treating them rather like a human xylophone. The problem, however, was that she had memorized each note by the color of each child's hair. According to her co-star, Theodore Bikel, when one of the children grew too big and had to be replaced, Martin demanded that the replacement have his or her hair dyed to match the color of the original child; otherwise, she could not possibly remember which head to pat. Still, the number was buoyant and fun and worked tremendously well in the show, as Maria and the children trooped up and down the living room, forming a confident and trusting bond between each other.

But they never left the living room.

That is, until the screenwriter, Ernest Lehman, opened up the number for the screen. In his earliest drafts, Lehman knew he wanted to place the number later in the movie and let it play all over the famous sights of Salzburg. Wise agreed; as he said forty years later on the Anniversary DVD, "In films, you get to do so much of the lyrics here, and you cut over here to another location, do the lyrics over there. That's the advantage of film. So when we had a chance to do that with 'Do Re Mi,' it just worked wonderfully well."

It was one thing to spring the musical number from its constraints on the proscenium stage in theory; the practice of it would take, well, quite a lot of practice. It fell to the film's choreographers, Marc Breaux and Dee Dee Wood, to begin the meticulous planning process. First, the song itself was rearranged to accommodate the various Salzburg locations; then Maurice Zuberano, the sketch artist for the production, created a large number of storyboards that matched the lyrics to the locations. Of course, rehearsing the choreography in Salzburg itself was a practical and financial impossibility, so the dancing sequences were created and rehearsed back on the Fox lot in Culver City.

PAGE 129: Near the finale, at the Mirabell Gardens.

LEFT: Maurice Zuberano's storyboards were the first attempt at breaking down the visuals for this complicated sequence, as the meadow picnic moves to the Winkler Terrace. Recognize the scene where the kids playfully pop in and out of the hedges? No? That's because the scene never made it past the storyboard stage.

ABOVE: Ernest Lehman's handwritten notes on the screenplay block out the various sequences.

DO - RE - MI - FA - SO - LA - TI - DO!

MARIA SINGS UNACCOMPANIED, REPEATED BY CHILDREN!

SO - DO - LA - FA - MI - DO - RE -

MARIA SINGS UNACCOMPANIED, REPEATED BY CHILDREN.

SO - DO - FA - TI - DO - RE - DO!

CHILDREN

SO - DO - LA - FA - ME - DO -

MARIA

WHEN YOU KNOW THE NOTES TO

CHILDREN

CHAPPELL PROF.

Eventually the choreography for "Do Re Mi" would be transferred to the nine separate Salzburg locations selected for the movie. (There were another seven locations chosen for a pre–"Do Re Mi" sequence, set to the music of "My Favorite Things.")

Marc Breaux and Saul Chaplin were sent ahead to Salzburg (it would be Chaplin's second trip) for the meticulous task of timing out the dance sequences at the locations. According to Wood in an interview for the fortieth anniversary DVD:

Mark and Saul went to Salzburg to time the length of the streets, the length of going here to there, and they were in the middle of the city and Mark was dancing in and out of traffic. Solly had his little tape recorder, playing back the music. Mark was dancing in and out and a policeman came up and spoke to them in German, asking what they were doing. They tried to explain and then finally the policeman said, "Well, where are you from?" Saul said, "America," and the policeman said, "Oh," and left.

PAGES 134–135: There are some things that only movies can do: a stunning location, a great cinematographer, and a spirited cast come together for a magic moment.

PAGES 132–133: Richard Rodgers' musical manuscript shows the simple, but effective, breakdown on the song's harmony. From left to right: The hills in Werfen; the meadow beneath the Untersberg; Winkler Terrace and two different spots in Mirabell Gardens—six of nine separate locations for "Do Re Mi," shot out of chronological sequence over the course of a month.

LEFT: In the Broadway version, Mary Martin makes friends with the von Trapp children by singing them the musical scale in the living room, soon after their first introductions.

ABOVE: Salzburg's cold cloudiness forced sunny smiles when sunny skies weren't available; the children huddle together between takes.

The genius moment was when Chaplin realized there were enough steps leading out of the Mirabell Gardens to accommodate the seven notes in the scale—one step for each note, then back down again for the final "do." That provided a neat and unforgettable finale for the number.

Back at the Fox lot in February, the choreographers began working out the sequences with Andrews and the seven children. Even the bicycling was worked out on the tiny streets separating the soundstages on the lot. As Wood put it, "The bicycles had to be rehearsed. Because if you notice, in one scene they're coming at the camera, straight on, and on certain notes where two kids would sing, their bikes would come forward and the other bikes would go back, then forward. They had to pace themselves so that they would stay in this formation." Before actual shooting began at the end of March, all of the musical numbers had been rehearsed and prerecorded.

It took ten shooting days over the course of a month to capture the sequences for "Do Re Mi," including several days when shooting was rained out. Only a director with Robert Wise's precise sense of editing could have constructed such a sequence so successfully. In addition to using the song to convey Maria's increased intimacy with the children, it gave her the opportunity to teach them how to sing after she had already earned their trust, which seems to be a more dramatically satisfying sequence of events. In the anniversary documentary, Julie Andrews explained that Lehman's transposition had an additional bonus: "He used it to signify a passage of time, so by the end of the song, the summer has passed. And Captain von Trapp is coming home with the Baroness. It's a lovely way of saying what fun we had during the summer. Filming that montage was probably for me the quintessential moment of the film."

The end of the song also gave Andrews a chance to add a signature moment of her own. In the Broadway version, Mary Martin, who had a particularly low register, dropped an octave on the song's final "do." But Andrews had her own magical vocal range. While climbing the stairs, she thought "how fun it might be to go higher—and higher and then higher. And so I asked if I could do the huge octave leap (actually I do it in half-octaves) and everybody said, 'Go for it' and that's sort of how it came about."

LEFT: The cast and crew at Winkler Terrace. Passers-by under the terrace kept hearing the playback of "Do Re Mi" broadcast on speakers and couldn't figure out what was going on.

ABOVE: Remember this sequence, in the middle of the "My Favorite Things" montage, where Liesl introduces Maria to her suitor, Rolf? No? That's because it was one of two scenes shot in Salzburg that Wise cut from the final movie. (The other was Christopher Plummer gazing wistfully at Maria's bedroom window.)

SOMETHING GOOD

LYRICS BY RICHARD RODGERS

Perhaps I had a wicked childhood,
Perhaps I had a mis'rable youth.
But somewhere in my wicked mis'rable past
There must have been a moment of truth.

For here you are,
Standing there,
Loving me,
Whether or not you should.

So, somewhere in my youth or childhood
I must have done something good.

Nothing comes from nothing,
Nothing ever could.
So, somewhere in my youth or childhood
I must have done something good.

For a leading romantic couple, Maria and the Captain have surprisingly little to sing to each other. In fact, confirming the real Maria von Trapp's assertion that she fell in love with the children, she has more to sing with them. But after Maria and the Captain confess their feelings for each other in the show's second act, a duet was a practical and emotional necessity. Hammerstein's words for "An Ordinary Couple" conjure up a world of simple domesticity, very much like a song he wrote in 1939 with Jerome Kern, "The Folks Who Live on the Hill":

> An ordinary couple
> Is all we'll ever be,
> For all I want of living
> Is to keep you close to me;
> To laugh and weep together
> While time goes on its flight,
> To kiss you every morning
> And to kiss you every night…
>
> An ordinary couple,
> Across the years we'll ride,
> Our arms around each other,
> And our children by our side.

When the movie was going into production, screenwriter Ernest Lehman voted to eliminate the song, and his opinion was seconded by director Robert Wise and Associate Producer Saul Chaplin. They met with Richard Rodgers in New York and diplomatically brought up their concerns about the song. Rodgers concurred immediately; in fact, he said, if they had had more time, and Hammerstein were in better health, they would have replaced the song out of town. "She's a nun who renounced her vows and he's a decorated naval captain—what's so ordinary about that?" he felt.

Rodgers was more than willing to try his own hand at crafting lyrics as well as music for a new song, and the movie's creative team was thrilled with the results. By 1964, Rodgers had written music and lyrics for some new songs for a movie remake of *State Fair,* and had a considerable hit with an original Broadway musical in 1962, *No Strings,* for which he created both music and lyrics to some of the best romantic duets of his entire career. Perhaps on a roll from that assignment, Rodgers concocted something simple, sincere, and charming with "Something Good." (Rodgers even manages a sly inversion of King Lear's line: "Nothing will come of nothing.") He also had the added muse of writing a melody specifically for Julie Andrews, a task he had performed so beautifully before in the 1957 television special of *Cinderella.* (He was less lucky with the other song assigned to him by Lehman and company—"I Have Confidence" had to go through several drafts and eventually required a final revision by Saul Chaplin.)

Still, if writing "Something Good" was a comparatively easy task, performing it for the movie was not. The gazebo setting had been reassembled back on the Fox lot, and its many glass panels required the director of photography, Ted McCord, to employ complicated lighting effects. He positioned some extremely powerful, old-fashioned Kleig lights to point directly downward along the columns of the gazebo. Unfortunately, the Kleig lights worked by shooting carbon arcs against each other and they made a terrible flatulent sound every time they were fired up. This noise sent Andrews into gales of laughter, while Christopher Plummer started giggling at the idea of the Captain and Maria proclaiming their eternal love for each other nose to nose. "I could see your eyes squeeze down into little f-stops," recalled Andrews in the 2005 reunion documentary. The two of them lost it. Wise called "Cut!" and set up the cameras again. Frrrrrmpff! went the carbon arcs, and the giggling began all over again. Wise called a two-hour lunch break, prevailing upon the actors to curb their "unprofessional idiotic laughing." Once lunch was over, it was back to the set and again the carbon arcs made their flatulent sound. More laughter. Wise, normally the most patient of professionals, threw up his hands—after all, by this time he was behind schedule—and decided to shoot the entire sequence in silhouette, so the camera would not catch his stars' childish misbehavior. It turned out to be a happy accident.

Whatever childhoods Andrews and Plummer might have had, they were certainly wicked that day on the Fox lot.

PAGE 141: *Julie Andrews and Christopher Plummer, framed in the hastily contrived silhouette that did so much to enhance the scene—and keep their giggling from showing up on camera.*

LEFT: *Theodore Bikel and Mary Martin sing "An Ordinary Couple" from the original stage version.*

CHAPTER SEVEN

AROUND THE WORLD

Was it just a coincidence that the first signs of the immense success of *The Sound of Music* would be seen in—of all places—Oklahoma?

Robert Wise and his crew returned to Hollywood at the beginning of July 1964 and managed to finish filming within eight comparatively uneventful weeks. (Christopher Plummer was not happy to discover he was going to be dubbed after all and Charmian Carr crashed through a piece of plate glass during her dance number, but that was about it.) Wise was relieved to escape the vagaries of location shooting, and control the vast array of Hollywood craftsmanship that the Fox Studios had to offer. After the footage was edited by William Reynolds, under the unerring gaze of Wise, and underscored by Irwin Kostal, the movie was ready to be shown to a preview audience.

Every producer takes a different approach to screening a preview of a rough cut. Some ignore the process entirely, but for those who do not, location—as in real estate—is of prime importance. Richard Zanuck and Wise selected two family-friendly locations in the Midwestern United States—Tulsa, Oklahoma, and Minneapolis, Minnesota—and held the screenings in early February. The results transcended even the wildest dreams of the most optimistic Hollywood mogul. The combined tally of score cards from the audience was incredible: Fair—0, Good—5, Excellent—460. Clearly this was an unprecedented state of affairs and Fox executives, who had shelled out the not-inconsiderable sum of $5.5 million on their screen musical, breathed a collective sigh of relief. If the review card scores were to be trusted, the movie could become that great and rare commodity in the entertainment world—a phenomenon.

As long as the movie reviewers liked it, too, of course.

When the movie critics filed their reviews during the first week of March 1965 (the Los Angeles opening gala was scheduled eight days later, on March 10), Wise and Richard Zanuck were astonished. *The Sound of Music* received a critical drubbing from the major East Coast critics, which made the Broadway opening-night notices seem like a round of nosegays. Bosley Crowther of the *New York Times* wrote that the movie was "staged by Mr. Wise in a cosy-cum-corny fashion that even theater people know is old hat." Judith Crist of the *New York Herald Tribune* weighed in with "this [icky-sticky movie] is for the five-to-seven set and their mommies who think their kids aren't up to the stinging sophistication and biting wit of *Mary Poppins*."

Even worse was a review written by Pauline Kael for *McCall's*, a genial magazine that catered to suburban housewives. According to Kael, the movie was "a sugar-coated lie that people seem to want to eat . . . Wasn't there perhaps one little von Trapp who didn't want to sing his head off . . . or who got nervous and threw up if he had to get on a stage?" *McCall's* readers thought Kael was so out of touch with their tastes that they demanded she be fired; she was. She was also soon hired as the movie critic for the *New Yorker*, where, in the witty words of her eventual successor on the film beat, Anthony Lane, "she remained supreme for the next quarter of a century, thus proving that *The Sound of Music* is so saintly that it confers a happy ending on all who touch its hem, even those of little faith."

Moviegoers around the country had plenty of faith, however. In its initial month-long engagement, *The Sound of Music* played in only twenty-five theaters nationwide in what was then called a "road show" roll-out—reserved tickets in advance, two showings a day, a souvenir program, an actual intermission—in an attempt to convey a Broadway kind of prestige on the picture. Even in this limited engagement, the movie quickly became number one at the box office. By the end of 1965, *The Sound of Music* had earned $50 million in box-office receipts— already a $30 million net profit. Within a year of its release, it had passed *Gone with the Wind* as the most successful picture of all time, an honor it held until *The Godfather* won the crown in 1972. As of January 1, 2006, *The Sound of Music* had grossed $163 million at the box office, and sat at number 119 in a list of all-time box-office champs, having been pushed to the back of the line by the

deluge of action/science fiction/comic book juggernauts of late twentieth-century cinema. However, when *The Sound of Music's* theatrical box-office receipts were adjusted for inflation in 2005, it ranked number 3 among all Hollywood movies, trumped only by *Gone with the Wind* and *Star Wars*.

As they say, living well is the best revenge, and winning a few Oscars does not hurt, either. *The Sound of Music* was nominated for ten Academy Awards and, on April 20 , 1966, the movie took home five statuettes. Robert Wise was honored as Best Director, as was Irwin Kostal (Best Scoring of Music, Adaptation or Treatment), William Reynolds (Best Film Editing), and James Corcoran and Fred Hynes (Best Sound). Finally, Jack Lemmon announced that *The Sound of Music* had won for Best Picture, making it— along with its rival *My Fair Lady*—the only musical to win both the Tony and the Oscar. Saul Chaplin accepted on Wise's behalf—the director was stuck in Hong Kong, having finally got *The Sand Pebbles* rolling in front of cameras. Julie Andrews was nominated for Best Actress but lost to Julie Christie (for *Darling*). Andrews took her loss with equanimity; she had won the award a year earlier, for *Mary Poppins*. Far more disappointing to her and the rest of the crew was the fact that Ernest Lehman, whose initial faith and expert craftsmanship had been so essential to the movie's existence, was not even nominated for an award.

When *The Sound of Music* was sold to the movies in 1960, there was a provision that the picture could not be released before December 1964 so that it would not intrude on potential theatrical box office. The Broadway version had closed a year before the movie opened, but the movie's success not only did not dampen future revivals of the show, it encouraged them. According to R&H Theatricals, the organization that licences the stage version, during the half-century since *The Sound of Music* opened on Broadway, there have been nearly 20,000 productions and there are still more than 500 productions staged every year in America, from major regional theater circuits to high school auditoriums. In the 1960s and 1970s, *The Sound of Music* was particularly popular in the summer theater circuit, and the role of Maria was played by such varied and talented ladies as Florence Henderson (who took the role on several times in repertory), Shirley Jones (another Rodgers and Hammerstein leading lady turned television mom), Barbara Cook, Roberta Peters, Barbara Eden, and Constance Towers (who is also one of several actresses to

PAGE 144: *Charmian Carr bids farewell to Nicholas Hammond; the Pan Am shoulder bag was a sure sign that travel was in order—Carr would stay in Salzburg after the company returned to Los Angeles to film a travelog, sponsored by—surprise!—Pan Am, among others.*

PAGES 146–147: *A widescreen version of the famous poster for the movie*

ABOVE: *No matter what the language, the song is the same: The Sound of Music, clockwise from top left: French, Croatian, Romanian, Japanese, Portuguese, and Spanish.*

play both Maria and Anna in *The King and I*—as were Marie Osmond and Maureen McGovern).

Still, for all its success around the country during the 1960s and 1970s, a major stage revival had eluded *The Sound of Music*. It was not until 1981 that such a production was attempted, and it occurred in London. The first British production had run two years past the opening of the movie, so West End audiences had been deprived of the show for only fourteen years. Ross Taylor, an ambitious producer who had scored a big success with *The King and I* the previous season, brought the musical back in style to the Apollo Victoria Theatre. He prevailed upon Petula Clark, the most successful female pop singer in British history, to play the role of Maria. Clark had initial reservations—she had never appeared in a stage musical and, frankly, she had just cleared the hurdle of fifty. Taylor convinced her to sign on and also hired June Bronhill, the Australian soprano with the glorious voice, to play the Mother Abbess (Bronhill would be the first actress to play both Maria and the Mother Abbess professionally).

Clark had the personal triumph of her career, winning over the difficult British critics who carped about the play's sugary sentimentality, and earning glorious reviews. She extended her six-month contract to thirteen months, playing at 101 percent capacity every week for more than a year. One week of her engagement set the West End record for highest weekly box office of all time.

One audience member who enjoyed Clark's performance more than the rest was Maria von Trapp. She attended the opening night (yes, she stood at Clark's curtain call) and proclaimed Taylor's production to be the best she had ever seen. It was hard to begrudge Maria her moment in the sun; since the movie producers had turned their backs on her (she was not even invited to the movie's premiere), her fame had been fleeting. Maria made some television appearances: her identity was guessed by Kitty Carlisle Hart on *To Tell the Truth* (it was not that difficult—Kitty had been at the Broadway opening-night party with Maria) and she appeared with Julie Andrews on her London-based variety program in 1973.

Throughout the 1970s, Maria had mostly devoted herself to the Trapp Family Lodge in Stowe, Vermont. She somewhat reluctantly turned over its day-to-day management to her son, Johannes, but she still continued as the hostess with the mostest, greeting visitors, signing autographs, and generally infusing the place with her good cheer and indomitability. Then, the week before Christmas in 1980, a bizarre and unpredictable fire broke out at the Lodge, just as the family was preparing for its seasonal arrivals. Within hours, the main complex had burned to the ground. One guest was killed (the freezing cold made rescue efforts nearly impossible) and most of Maria's personal effects, papers, and memorabilia were lost. A bit of Maria's personal spark was lost in the fire as well. Under Johannes' astute management, the Lodge was not only rebuilt from the ashes, but was tripled in size and maximized in terms of comfort, amenities, and efficiency, including a hundred time-share units. When the

ABOVE: One of the stranger recordings of all time: In 1959, members of the Trapp Family Singers reunited (supplemented by additional singers), under the guidance of Father Wasner to record the music to The Sound of Music. It lacks a certain, shall we say, showbiz finesse and is a bit like having Mozart come back from the beyond to play the soundtrack to Amadeus.

RIGHT: Petula Clark's West End debut as a leading actress was a smash, and was the first major revival of the show—on either side of the Atlantic—since the original production.

OPPOSITE, CLOCKWISE FROM TOP LEFT: Marie Osmond brought her ebullience to the character of Maria for several American tours; Liz Robertson's heart is blessed with the sound of music in a highly successful 1992 British tour that appeared at Sadler's Wells; the Japanese production in 1965, as Maria teaches the children "Do Re Mi."

ABOVE: Rebecca Luker teaches the children the musical scales without ever once going on a picnic or riding a bicycle in the 1998 Broadway revival; for a 1977 tour, the Rodgers and Hammerstein movie star and television mom, Shirley Jones, brought along her valise and guitar. Eagle-eyed readers will notice the teenaged Sarah Jessica Parker, third from the right.

ABOVE: *In 1990,* The Sound of Music *made a return to New York—to the New York City Opera—directed by the lyricist's son, James Hammerstein.* *Laurence Guittard and Debby Boone, who recorded the pop hit* You Light Up My Life, *dance the Laendler.*

phœnix-like Trapp Family Lodge re-emerged in January 1984, Maria was delighted to share the opening festivities with her old friend, Mary Martin. But even Maria von Trapp's energy was waning, and on March 28, 1987, she passed away at Stowe; she lies buried next to the grave of her beloved captain, Georg von Trapp. Martin said, "Maria didn't just climb over that mountain, she helped everybody over it!"

Three years later, Martin left the scene as well, marking the end of the old guard. Rodgers had passed away late in 1979, Russel Crouse in 1966. Howard Lindsay, who never thought *The Sound of Music* had a snowball's chance of making more than $12 million (it did so within months of its opening), died in 1968, but not before letting off one last riposte to the press. Responding to a *Times* article about the money-making prowess of *The Sound of Music*, he wrote: "Much has been written about the success of *The Sound of Music* play and motion picture. Is it immodest of me to point out, because no one else *ever* does, that Russel Crouse and I had a hand in it?"

The original book by Lindsay and Crouse got its first major Broadway revival in 1998, ironically on March 12, sixty years to the day that Hitler marched into Austria. From the mid-1980s on, most of the major shows of Broadway's golden age had been given first-class revivals. Three of Oscar Hammerstein's shows—*Carousel*, *Show Boat*, and *The King and I*—were restaged in particularly persuasive new interpretations. The time was simply right for *The Sound of Music*. Rebecca Luker, a well-regarded Broadway performer, was given the starring role in this revival and, although the production was, by and large, a traditional presentation of the material, the design of the show displayed considerable respect for Austrian traditions. The production also confronted the Nazi menace head-on; the Nazi flag, with its black-spider swastika, was firmly in evidence during the show's finale at the Festival. (To be fair, the swastika first appeared during the Festival sequence in a British revival at Sadler's Wells in 1992, starring Liz Robertson and Christopher Cazenove.) *The Sound of Music* suffered the usual slings and arrows from the *New York Times*: "On one level, it will always nauseate," wrote Ben Brantley. One can only be grateful that the *Herald Tribune* ceased publication decades ago. The revival ran a year and a half.

Perhaps the most exciting part of the Broadway revival was its opening night, when four of the surviving von

ABOVE: Florence Henderson picks up her guitar two decades after heading the national tour; Jon Voight, of Midnight Cowboy and Deliverance fame, began his career as a delivery boy. He replaced Rolf in the original Broadway The Sound of Music. Here he sings with Marissa Mason.

ABOVE: The largest reunion of the von Trapp Family—real and fictional—ever assembled. Here, on the stage of the Martin Beck Theater at the 1998 revival of The Sound of Music, are: (Top row, left to right) Eleonore, Agathe, Werner, Maria, Rosmarie, and Johannes von Trapp. (Top of middle) Dennis Parlato (replacement for Michael Siberry) and Rebecca Luker. (Middle, left to right) The movie children, all grown up: Kym Karath, Debbie Turner, Angela Cartwright,

Duane Chase, Heather Menzies, Nicholas Hammond, and Charmian Carr. (Bottom row) The children from the revival.

RIGHT: Admiration, respect, and a discreet attraction have made Christopher Plummer and Julie Andrews friends and colleagues for over forty years. This 2005 picture was taken in conjunction with the 40th Anniversary release of the DVD of The Sound of Music.

Trapp children—Johannes, Maria, Agathe, and Rosmarie—attended the premiere. Later that year, they were joined by their brother Werner and sister Eleonore in New York City, when the governor of the Austrian State of Salzburg presented them with the Golden Decoration of Honor, the region's highest civilian honor. At the ceremony, there was also an appearance from the entire group of seven actors who played the children in the movie—their first reunion in over a decade. If that was not enough, both camps trooped over to the Martin Beck Theater to see a performance of the revival, and all three families took an unprecedented curtain call. One can certainly bet that Maria von Trapp would have stood up for that one.

By the end of the twentieth century, the breadth and scope of *The Sound of Music*'s influence was enormous. After it opened in America, the movie was immediately dubbed in four languages, and has subsequently played all over the world. In literal-minded Argentina, it is known as *The Rebellious Novice*; in the more poetic Hong Kong, it is called *Fairy Music Blow Fragrant Place, Place Hear*. After the millennium, there was a surprising jump in the number of high-profile professional stage productions all over the world. Such countries as Italy, Holland, Mexico, Sweden, Norway, and Israel presented local-language translations (in Israel, both nuns and Nazis performed the material in Hebrew). And, of course, several generations have experienced *The Sound of Music* on video or DVD, where it still remains one of the all-time unit-selling champs, with several special editions in release. For the fortieth anniversary release of the DVD, Fox enlisted the services of Julie Andrews to host and narrate a number of features, including a reunion with Christopher Plummer. Although Plummer's aversion to the movie is well-known, he has nothing but affection and respect for Andrews, and *The Sound of Music* fans have enjoyed their joint appearances over the last few years in a television version of *On Golden Pond* and a special Christmas event that toured the United States in 2002.

The reach of *The Sound of Music* extends farther and farther every year. In May 2004, an American production was mounted for the most extensive tour ever of a Western musical in Asia. The movie has a particular appeal for Chinese audiences; it is easily the most well-known Western musical in China. The tour began in Shanghai and Beijing, then extended to Taipei, Tokyo, and Osaka, then to South Korea and Singapore. Ted Chapin, president of the

Rodgers and Hammerstein Organization, reported that "*The Sound of Music* has become a calling card for the American musical . . . and audiences continue to be grabbed by its story of triumph over adversity, of human connections made with prescribed regimens. Watching it in this place, thousands of miles from home, made me appreciate once again the power of the show and the story that it tells."

It was inevitable that a story with that much power would inspire people to want to write themselves into it. There are certain phenomena in twentieth-century popular culture that invite fans to go beyond owning the DVD to becoming part of the mythology—*Star Trek* and *The Rocky Horror Picture Show* come readily to mind. The *Sing-a-Long Sound of Music* is a glorious mélange of all three. It began life as a one-night event at the London Gay and Lesbian Film Festival. One festival organizer had been visiting his grandmother at her nursing home in Scotland and the residents were watching the movie *Seven Brides for Seven*

Brothers and singing along with songs, following lyric sheets spread on their laps. If that less-than-brilliant movie musical could inspire such participation, he thought, why not the greatest movie musical of all time?

The London Festival presentation was so popular that the whole concept moved into the Prince Charles Cinema, a budget-minded theater off Leicester Square, in August 1999. The Prince Charles showed the film—with karaoke-style song-lyric subtitles—twice a week, on Friday nights and Sunday afternoons. Audiences soon packed the screenings and the showings started to tour England, then most of Europe and Australia to equally enthusiastic fans. In September 2000, the *Sing-a-Long* found a home at New York City's Ziegfeld Theater, then traveled to Chicago and every major city in America—including, of course, San Francisco, where its camp appeal was warmly embraced. The hills of Los Angeles were particularly alive with the sounds of the *Sing-a-Long*: the cavernous Hollywood Bowl hosted four annual showings, but one particular sultry evening in July 2005 was a very special event.

An audience of 18,000 packed the Bowl for a completely sold-out screening of the *Sing-a-Long Sound of Music*. Before the screening of the movie, there were the obligatory events that have accompanied the *Sing-a-Long* sensation since its London debut. A host whipped up enthusiasm from the audience (not difficult to do); there was a talent show in which the youthful descendants of the Trapp Family sang "Edelweiss"; and some surprises, including an appearance of the entire cast of children from the 1965 movie.

And then there are the costumes. Audience members for the *Sing-a-Long* are the farthest thing imaginable from couch potatoes—they come ready to sing (the movie is subtitled with all the lyrics to the songs), to hiss (poor Elsa Schraeder), to boo (the Nazis, of course), and to yell inappropriate comments (not surprisingly, the "Sixteen Going on Seventeen" number takes the brunt of those). And they come ready dressed as characters, lyrics, concepts—anything at all—mentioned in the movie.

The costumes worn by audience members get more baroque with every new city the *Sing-a-Long* conquers. In addition to the obvious girls in white dresses with blue satin sashes or the fellow who dressed all in bright yellow, as Ray, a drop of golden sun, there have been costumes that have strained credulity and taste—the gentlemen wearing overalls and brandishing a plunger as "Chris the Plumber" or the young lady festooned with a bevy of brown balloons who came as "The Lonely Goat Turd." At the Hollywood Bowl showing in 2005, the winner of the best costume competition was given quite a run for his money: a pair of drapes (later to be playclothes, of course), a quartet of very buxom ladies whose "hills" were quite lively, a little girl with a pale pink coat, and the inevitable bright copper kettles and warm woollen mittens. But the gentleman who received first prize (from Charmian Carr, no less—the fellow must have been delirious) was dressed as an eight-foot carburetor—as in the one that the nuns remove from the Nazis' car at the end of the picture.

When dusk fell, the main event of the evening began and the movie spooled along, just as it had for forty years—except now Julie Andrews' solo on the hilltop near Werfern was accompanied by the world's largest amateur choir. Perhaps the reverberating echoes could be heard at the Fox studios in Culver City where, five decades earlier, executives had once mocked the Broadway show's potential to emerge as a hit movie.

The loyal audiences who flock to the *Sing-a-Longs* and purchase their kits of fake edelweiss, cough drops, and foam-rubber nun puppets come not to bury *The Sound of Music* but to praise it. The crowds have a healthy reverence for the movie as well as a healthy lack of either cynicism or pomposity. The sheer earnestness of the enterprise can melt the heart of the sternest critic. As Anthony Lane noted in his 1999 *New Yorker* piece: "The atmosphere . . . was strangely unmocking, even its coarsest moments. . . . [*The Sound of Music*] offered one of the last breaths of innocence in American cinema. . . . That is why we go back to Wise's film; we all know better now, but most of us secretly wish that we didn't."

The breadth of the movie's message reached every corner of the globe and audiences opened up their hearts to its craftsmanship and good cheer. The only real holdout was the very country that gave birth to the whole shebang: Austria.

LEFT: Some Sing-a-Long participants: the carburetor won at the Hollywood Bowl in 2005; other contestants include Ray, a Drop of Golden Sun, and a nun who looks suspiciously like he needs a shave.

SIXTEEN GOING ON SEVENTEEN

You wait, little girl, on an empty stage
For fate to turn the light on.
Your life, little girl, is an empty page
That men will want to write on—
To write on.

You are sixteen, going on seventeen,
Baby, it's time to think.
Better beware,
Be canny and careful,
Baby, you're on the brink.

You are sixteen, going on seventeen,
Fellows will fall in line,
Eager young lads
And roués and cads
Will offer you food and wine.

Totally unprepared are you
To face a world of men.
Timid and shy and scared are you
Of things beyond your ken.

You need someone older and wiser
Telling you what to do . . .
I am seventeen, going on eighteen,
I'll take care of you.

I am sixteen, going on seventeen,
I know that I'm naïve.
Fellows I meet
May tell me I'm sweet
And willingly I believe.

I am sixteen, going on seventeen,
Innocent as a rose.
Bachelor dandies,
Drinkers of brandies—
What do I know of those?

Totally unprepared am I
To face the world of men.
Timid and shy and scared am I
Of things beyond my ken.

I need someone older and wiser
Telling me what to do . . .
You are seventeen, going on eighteen,
I'll depend on you.

PAGE 163: Charmian Carr going through her dance with someone who looks suspiciously like Daniel Truitthe's dance double. The gazebo walls are opened up for the shoot.

ABOVE: Brian Davies and Lauri Peters were Broadway's original "supporting couple." Peters and the other six children would be jointly nominated for a Tony Award.

When Rodgers and Hammerstein revolutionized the American musical in 1943 with *Oklahoma!*, they provided a satisfying structure for their shows. Most of them consisted of a main romantic plot and then, to diversify things, a comedic subplot. As they continued their collaboration into the 1950s, they varied the formula—sometimes the main plot would be platonic and confrontational and the subplot would become emotional and romantic, as in *The King and I*. While the main story of *The Sound of Music* is taken largely from factual biography, the subplot, that of the eldest von Trapp child, Liesl, falling in love with a young telegraph delivery boy, is the pure invention of Lindsay and Crouse. Although the Liesl/Rolf subplot allows for the emotional development of a young girl—always a good story, especially when the leading lady is in her early forties—it also sets up the spread of Nazism in the world surrounding the von Trapps.

Rolf's gradual endorsement of the Nazi Party is an important plot point and allows the audience to grasp Nazism not through a newsreel or abstract concept, but rather through a character's development instead. (This neat bit of dramaturgy was used seven years later in the musical *Cabaret*.) Rolf is even allowed the pangs of a youthful conscience—in the final scene, his flashlight catches Liesl hiding among her family, but he decides not to report the von Trapps to his superiors.

Of all the changes from the historical record made in the name of drama, the Liesl/Rolf subplot is the one that so stupefied the von Trapp Family that they could only laugh at it. After all, there was no daughter named Liesl, and the eldest von Trapp child was Rupert, a strapping, fifty-four-year-old Vermont physician when the movie was released. For years, when people asked Rupert which of the von Trapp children he was, he would point a finger into the dimple of his chin, curtsy, and say, "I'm Liesl!"

For the movie, "Sixteen Going on Seventeen" was the last musical number filmed in mid-August on the Fox studio lot. The gazebo where Rolf and Liesl share their first kiss (and first dance number) was re-created on the lot, after the original gazebo was left back in Salzburg. (One can still visit it, although it was moved from its original location to the grounds of Hellbrun Palace.) Charmian Carr, who played Liesl, had never sung or danced professionally before the movie. On the first day of filming the dance scene, she

was given a new pair of shoes without the traditional rubber-coated soles, and on the first take, Carr jumped on the bench and kept going through the plate-glass windows. "I thought Robert Wise was going to have a heart attack," she said. "His face just went white because he thought 'That's it, she's done for!' and he was probably figuring out 'How am I going to replace her?'"

Luckily Charmian had only sprained her ankle and it was quickly bandaged. The costume crew did what they could to cover the bandage with makeup, but to viewers with sharp eyesight, it was pretty apparent. However, in the recent DVD releases of *The Sound of Music*, the bandage has been digitally erased. Carr does not remember worrying much about the accident; far more bothersome to her was the age of her co-star, Daniel Truitthe. "I was twenty-one at the time, and he was younger than I—he was twenty. At twenty-one, you wouldn't dare date a man that was younger. So I had to pretend I liked him."

ABOVE: Dee Dee Wood's notes on the choreography for the song.

CHAPTER EIGHT

AND BACK TO VIENNA

The von Trapp family never sang in front of the Nazi high command. In fact, one of the reasons they were forced to flee Austria was because a high-ranking Nazi official suggested that it would please the führer if the Trapp Chamber Choir would sing at his forty-ninth birthday party, and Georg von Trapp refused. So, what were they doing on stage at the Salzburg Festival, singing in front of a giant swastika, while soldiers from the Wehrmacht were patroling the audience, guarding the leading Nazi Party official in Salzburg, who was watching the performance from the royal box?

This was not reality, of course. It was a bit of very effective dramatic licence courtesy of French-Canadian director Renaud Doucet. Doucet was hired to direct *The Sound of Music* at the Vienna Volksoper in February 2005. His directorial vision for the penultimate scene where the von Trapps perform at the Festival was a *coup de théâtre*: with the uniformed Nazi soldiers and blinding searchlights, it felt as if Austria were, once again, under Nazi occupation. A frisson was in the air—some backs stiffened, several people disapproved—but the reception from the audience at the curtain call was rapturous. The Volksoper ("people's opera") had pulled off a daring move, ironically, by deciding to produce one of the most commercially successful musicals ever written. Critics (as they always have and apparently always will) sniffed at the choice of material and its execution: "Not a single memorable melody," said one. ("In contradiction to the views of about 50 million people," responded Rudolph Berger, the artistic director of the Volksoper and the person responsible for choosing *The Sound of Music* for the repertory.) The Volksoper production, performed entirely in German, quickly sold out its twenty-two-performance run, then added more than thirty performances and sold those out as well. Under the baton of the Cincinnati Pops' resident maestro, Erich Kunzel, fifty-three musicians—including an organist—sent the songs of Rodgers and Hammerstein soaring majestically out of the orchestra pit and into the air of Vienna.

It would be thrilling to report that *The Sound of Music* had returned in triumph to Vienna, the birthplace of Maria Kutschera, but that would be slightly inaccurate.

It had never been performed there at all.

The problems with the reception of *The Sound of Music* in Austria (and, by extension, its neighbor to the north, Germany) started at the very beginning. When Robert Wise was filming in Salzburg in 1964, he encountered immediate resistance from the town fathers about depicting the *Anschluss*. The suggestion that he might film Nazi soldiers marching through the city, festooned with banners emblazoned with swastikas, was horrifying to the Salzburg authorities, and they refused. Wise countered by suggesting he cut to actual newsreels of the Austrians embracing Hitler. That turned things around quickly, and a compromise was reached whereby a garrison of soldiers marched through the Residenzplatz, framed by one lonely Nazi banner in the background. It was simple but effective. (One can only imagine what William Wyler, had he made the movie, would have done with this sequence.)

What infuriated Wise, however, were not the negotiations for this sequence, but the subsequent actions by Fox's Munich branch manager once the movie was released in West Germany in 1965, with the title *Meine Lieder, Meine Traume* ("My Song, My Dream"). The branch manager thought the movie would play better if it ended right after the wedding between the Captain and Maria: pan up to the bells of Mondsee Cathedral tolling joyously, fade out, roll the credits, and just skip all that unpleasantness of the Nazis marching into Salzburg. When Wise heard that the movie had been released this way in Germany, he exploded and, to their credit, so did the executives at Fox. The branch manager was quickly sacked and the original cut of the movie was restored. Beyond the principle of the thing, it hardly mattered; the movie bombed in Germany, and played only a miserable three weeks in Salzburg.

The fact is, neither Germany nor Austria has ever taken to *The Sound of Music* in any form. Beyond its initial three-week run in 1965, the movie has barely existed in Austria; it was not until Christmas 2000 that Austrian State Broadcasting had even shown the movie on television, and the stage version had never appeared, with the exception of a brief parody version, until the Volksoper version in 2005.

There have been several reasons bruited about for this conspicuous absence. One is that *The Sound of Music* is simply bringing salt to Salzburg; in other words, it is an Americanized (and thereby assumed to be a coarsened) portrayal of Austrian culture. "It's a view of Austria unknown to people in this country," said Rudolph Berger. "Nobody knew *The Sound of Music* but everybody knew about it." Indeed, some of the musical's broad outlines of history and culture could be seen as, if not offensive, certainly not well-researched. (The Volksoper made one crucial rectifying change by substituting "Schnitzel with noodles" to "Gulasch mit Nockerln," which is far more accurate.) It is not surprising that there is a prejudice against the piece because of its popularity and its point of view. Renaud Doucet, the Volksoper director, said, "*The Sound of Music* is often seen as kitsch, but it reminds us that freedom is something we have to fight for every day; there's no kitsch in that." Native cultures will often resist foreign interpretations of their legends and history; the Danny Kaye movie *Hans Christian Andersen* was totally disregarded in Andersen's native Denmark, and London violently dismissed the first production of Stephen Sondheim's *Sweeney Todd* as a Broadway-ization of a story that every British schoolchild knew by heart.

Austrians have also claimed that they already had a perfectly good movie version of the von Trapp story—two perfectly good movie versions, in fact: *Die Trapp Familie* and *Die Trapp Familie in Amerika*. The two movies were even re-released theatrically in Austria to great success as late as 1985. But the fictional von Trapps were better known in Austria than their actual counterparts; among the few Austrians who knew the full von Trapp story, there were some, according to Rudolph Berger, who harbored a certain resentment toward the von Trapps for leaving the country, while others had to stay through the turmoil of the Nazi occupation.

Which brings one to the third reason: the role of Nazism in the von Trapp story. According to a director of the

PAGE 166: *The Salzburg Festival scene performed by the Vienna Volksoper; the brazen reference to the Nazis made audiences sit up and take notice of both the show and their common history.*

PAGES 168–169: *The stunning finale of the Volksoper: the von Trapps face an uncertain future.*

RIGHT: *The city fathers of Salzburg conceded the brief use of the Residenzplatz for the filming of the Anschluss for the movie— no cheering crowds were allowed, however.*

Salzburg Festival, Helga Rabl-Stadler, "When we deal with our past, there are always two groups in Austria. One group ignores it, doesn't want to know, and the other group wants to talk about it in a serious way." One could not argue for long that *The Sound of Music* deals with the Third Reich in a serious way, but it does present a story that opens up the issue for discussion. Continuing, Rabl-Stadler says, "It is one way to tell young people, 'The time was like this.'" A very good place to start.

Despite the general apathy on the part of the average good citizen of Austria toward *The Sound of Music*, it certainly has not hurt the tourist business, especially in Salzburg. Out of one million annual tourists, more than 300,000 people journey there specifically because of *The Sound of Music*. Three-quarters of all the American tourists who travel there do so because of the sights and sounds of the movie (as do tourists from all over the world, particularly England and, more recently, Japan). Frommer's *Budget Travel* magazine named Salzburg as the number one movie-related travel site in the world.

There is certainly enough for a Maria-minded tourist to do in Salzburg. As early as 1966, when American Express set up the first *Sound of Music* tour, there have been tour buses, guides, and all-day excursions to more than a dozen different locations featured in the movie. Since 1972, Panorama Tours has been the leading tour organization in Salzburg, taking nearly 50,000 customers a year on its various *Sound of Music* tours. Stefan Herzl, head of Panorama, said, "On our tour we try to bring visitors closer to the city and its surroundings, so you can separate fact from fiction. The more you immerse yourself in the world of Salzburg, the more you love this story." The very first *Sing-a-Long Sound of Music* to appear in Salzburg had a successful engagement—which would be repeated—in summer 2005. There is even serious discussion of building a von Trapp Museum in the center of the city.

In the end, *The Sound of Music* appears capable of melting any heart—or, at the very least, making its presence known as an unstoppable international phenomenon. As Maria says before she begins her journey to the von Trapp villa, "When the Lord closes a door, somewhere He opens a window." In the continuing saga of *The Sound of Music*, there appear to be far more windows than doors, and inspired artists around the world are flinging them wide open all the time.

ABOVE: *Johanna von Trapp painted this blossoming of Austria's most revered flower; Christopher Plummer sings of it, right.*

"WHEN THE LORD CLOSES A DOOR,
SOMEWHERE HE OPENS A WINDOW."
MARIA

EDELWEISS

Edelweiss,
Edelweiss,
Every morning you greet me.
Small and white,
Clean and bright,
You look happy to meet me.

Blossom of snow,
May you bloom and grow,
Bloom and grow forever—

Edelweiss,
Edelweiss,
Bless my homeland forever.

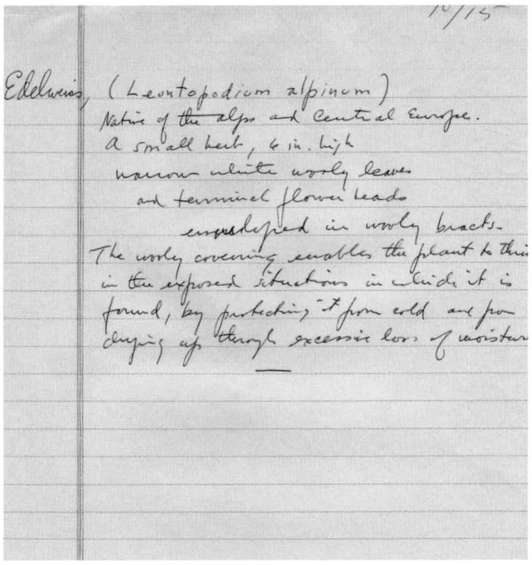

10/15

Edelweiss (Leontopodium alpinum)
Native of the Alps and central Europe.
A small herb, 6 in. high
narrow white woolly leaves
and terminal flower heads
enveloped in woolly bracts.
The woolly covering enables the plant to thrive
in the exposed situations in which it is
found, by protecting it from cold and from
drying up through excessive loss of moisture.

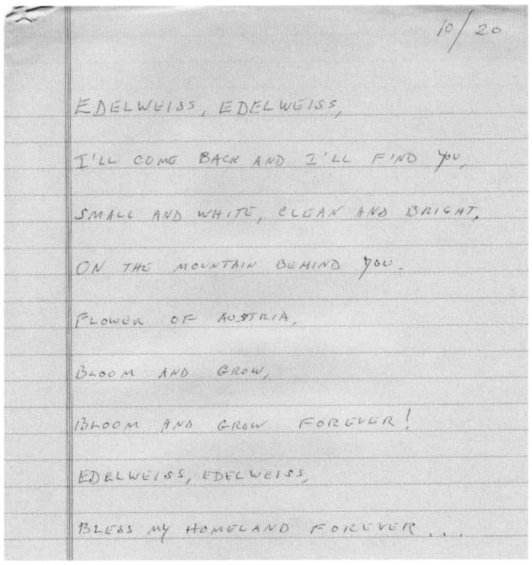

10/20

EDELWEISS, EDELWEISS,

I'LL COME BACK AND I'LL FIND YOU,

SMALL AND WHITE, CLEAN AND BRIGHT,

ON THE MOUNTAIN BEHIND YOU.

FLOWER OF AUSTRIA,

BLOOM AND GROW,

BLOOM AND GROW FOREVER!

EDELWEISS, EDELWEISS,

BLESS MY HOMELAND FOREVER...

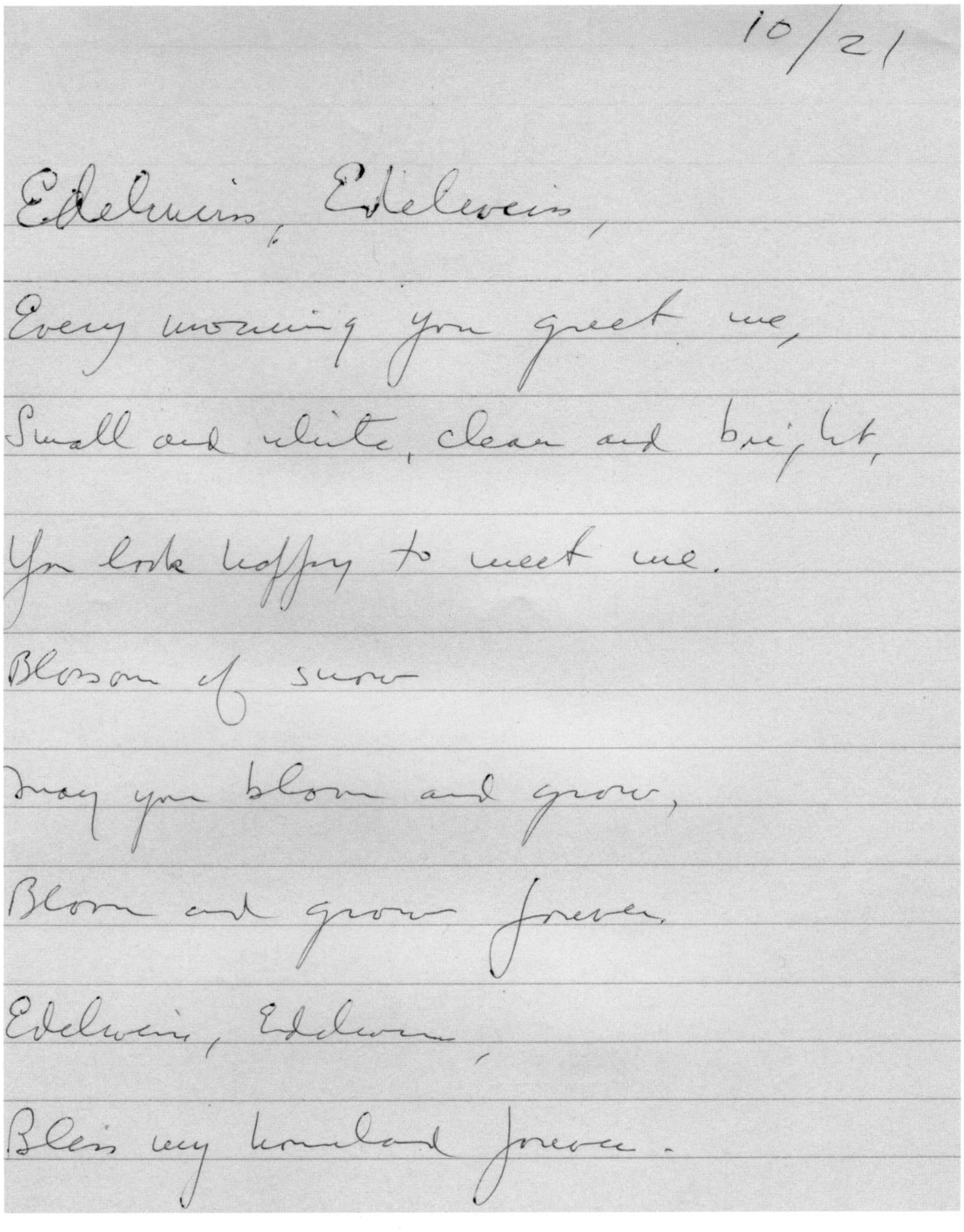

10/21

Edelweiss, Edelweiss,

Every morning you greet me,

Small and white, clean and bright,

You look happy to meet me.

Blossom of snow

May you bloom and grow,

Bloom and grow forever,

Edelweiss, Edelweiss,

Bless my homeland forever.

When *The Sound of Music* had its out-of-town tryout in the fall of 1959, it was a nearly perfect show in the hands of master craftsmen. Normally, a show might undergo a radical revision in a town like Boston, but, musically, at least, there was only one significant change to the song list.

It was felt that Theodore Bikel, a natural and accomplished folksinger, could use a moment with his guitar; it would be particularly effective if his character sang something late in the show about the land that he loved. Ironically, during the Boston tryout of Rodgers and Hammerstein's first show, *Oklahoma!*, in 1943, the producer asked Oscar Hammerstein for a new song in the second act, something that would articulate the characters' love for their land. In that case, he obliged with the title number. For *The Sound of Music*, he spent the second week in Boston crafting "Edelweiss" as a song for Captain von Trapp to sing at the Festival competition. The song's patriotic resonance created a bittersweet atmosphere for the von Trapp family's departure and audiences were moved as well.

Because of Hammerstein's illness and late arrival to Boston, Rodgers—departing from the customary sequence of their collaboration—wrote the music first. As one can see from his handwritten notes, Hammerstein first did some basic research about the flower, the native-grown emblem of Austria. Within the course of a week, he gradually moved to something more poetic and sincerely touching in its direct simplicity. With the exception of some last-minute tweaks in the nuns' opening song, those lyrics were the last words Oscar Hammerstein would ever craft for the musical stage.

For the movie version, Lehman followed the lead from a line in the original libretto and moved the song earlier in the story, allowing the Captain to show a softer (and more musical) side to his children. Christopher Plummer was not terribly pleased at the assignment: "I hate the guitar! I practiced until my fingers bled. I was trained on the piano—that's my instrument." He also had cause to be frustrated by his own vocal instrument. When he was offered the part of the Captain, Plummer was told that his singing would be dubbed—and he immediately turned down the role. After prolonged negotiations, a compromise was reached among Wise, Saul Chaplin, and Plummer; he would be assigned a singing coach, record his own vocals, and when the movie went into post-production, they could determine whether or not his singing was up to the demands of the movie. Alas, the production team eventually decided that, despite Plummer's hard work, he would have to be dubbed. Director Wise diplomatically suggested to Plummer that his singing was undermining the fine work he was doing in the acting department; he graciously relented to have his voice dubbed by Bill Lee. (Plummer's singing didn't seem to bother the Tony Awards voters nine years later when he was named Best Actor in a Musical for *Cyrano*, performing seven songs a night...)

Lehman kept the original setting of "Edelweiss," during the Festival competition, but Wise was able to expand the reach of the scene by having the Captain, clearly moved by his own imminent departure from his homeland, ask the assembled crowd to join in the anthem with him. The moment owes something to the singing of "La Marseillaise" in the movie *Casablanca*—in both cases, the Nazis glower ineffectually as the chorus of native patriotism swells around them.

"Edelweiss" has evoked so much patriotic feeling that in 1984, the Reagan White House supposedly thought the song was, in fact, the actual Austrian national anthem and had the song played to honor Austrian president Rudolf Kirchschlager during a state visit. As one of the honored guests at the White House dinner that night was the Baroness Maria von Trapp—aged seventy-nine—one supposes the lapse could be forgiven.

As the fictional Maria reminds us, the very beginning is a very good place to start. A very good place to end would be with the final words written by one of the masters of the lyrical arts, Oscar Hammerstein.

PAGE 175: Christopher Plummer takes center stage at Rock Riding School to lead his countrymen in a patriotic anthem.

LEFT: Three drafts of "Edelweiss": Hammerstein's notes on the actual flower; a nearly perfect penultimate draft; and the final version, more abstract and less specific, but still a lovely piece of poetry and Hammerstein's last full lyric for the stage.

A LONG, LONG WAY TO RUN

Way back when, before one note of *The Sound of Music* was written, the challenge was for a star—Mary Martin—to find the right vehicle. Fifty years later, for the first major English-language stage revival of the 21st century, the challenge was for the vehicle to find the right star.

Taking up the challenge was one of the leading lights of the modern musical theater: Andrew Lloyd Webber. When he was thirteen, Lloyd Webber wrote a fan letter to Richard Rodgers prior to the West End premiere of *The Sound of Music*. Rodgers was kind enough to meet with him and arrange for a ticket for opening night. Decades later, Lloyd Webber had become the most popular living composer of theatrical music and had founded The Really Useful Group, his own production company. As early as 2000, *The Sound of Music* had begun to stimulate Lloyd Webber's producing instinct. As he said in an interview, 'Wouldn't it be great to do a version of *The Sound of Music* with a girl who really was getting onto eighteen, who could really climb a tree and scrape her knee."

Lloyd Webber contacted the Rodgers and Hammerstein Organization in New York about the possibility of his producing a new London version of *The Sound of Music* and was given the green light. Other projects took priority, but things looked particularly promising in early 2006, when it seemed as if Lloyd Webber had found the perfect star for his vehicle: movie actress Scarlett Johansson. The twenty-one-year-old starlet Johansson "gave an impromptu rendition of songs from the hit movie in front of a restaurant full of people to prove her singing credentials and obsession with the musical," according to Lloyd Webber, "but it wasn't to be." Apparently, in addition to musical chops, Johansson also had a movie star's needs and sheaf of commitments.

And so, Lloyd Webber and his coproducer on the project, David Ian, decided to do a 180-degree reversal. "I said to David, if we can't get a star, I don't want to abandon [the project], so we'll just have to make a star." They would turn to a unique twenty-first century phenomenon to find their Maria: the television reality-show talent search. Plucking an unknown out of nowhere would prove to be a controversial decision, but, ultimately a popular and successful one—another triumph for Lord Lloyd Webber.

After all, isn't *The Sound of Music* the story of a novice who has to make a good impression on an older man with an aristocratic title?

Although *The Sound of Music* has been embraced by audiences all over the world, it has a special relationship with theatergoers in the UK. The original West End run of the show ran hundreds of performances longer than its Broadway counterpart; since then, London has seen two successful major revivals and the worldwide phenomenon of the *Sing-a-long Sound of Music* was launched in England. There was sure to be a massive audience for the reality show, inevitably titled *How Do You Solve a Problem Like Maria?* and broadcast on BBC1.

Maria would be the first talent competition related to a theatrical (as opposed to a pop) venture, and by July of 2006, BBC1 had moved the pieces quickly and efficiently into place. The series would be broadcast in eight parts, on Saturday evenings, culminating in a September 16 program that would anoint a Maria in front of an eventual viewership of nearly eight million viewers. The winner would be guaranteed a six-month contract to play the lead in a West End run of *The Sound of Music*—an unprecedented opportunity. Small wonder, then, that thousands of potential Marias poured forth from all corners of the UK and from a host of occupations—professional singers to police officers— each willing and eager for the chance to embody their child- hood heroine. As one hopeful contestant averred, she was a natural for Maria because she also loved children, sang on the way to work, and "fancied Christopher Plummer."

These battalions of Marias had to face a judging panel composed of three stalwarts of the British Theater: Zoe Tyler, a premier vocal coach for stage and pop singers; John Barrowman, American-raised actor/singer and West End musical star; and David Ian, chairman of global theater at Live Nation and one of the West End's most prolific producers, who was investing along with Lloyd Webber in the production itself. Ian's main concern was that the new Maria would exude that rare characteristic—"star quality"— or, as he put it less grandiosely, that she could "put bums on seats." Lording it over the three judges, as it were, was Andrew Lloyd Webber himself, exercising an executive privilege; the rules of the competition initially permitted him to "save" one of the two lowest scoring Marias per week, no matter how the television audience voted.

The judges whittled down the thousands of applicants to fifty-four contestants who were then sent to be trained at "Maria School," an academy constructed solely for producing viable Austrian governesses with guitar. (Actually, fifty were selected by the judges, but Lloyd Webber, having screened the contestants' videos privately, added several of his own choices.) Eventually, twenty of those fifty-four girls would be sent to Lloyd Webber's private theater on his estate in Sydmonton to perform before an invited audience, and, out of those twenty, through much discussion and horse-trading between Lloyd Webber and the judges, ten finalists moved on to the part of the selection process where the television audience voted for their favorite.

One of the more refreshing by-products of the competition was a chance to investigate just who "Maria (Rainer) von Trapp" actually is. As anyone who saw *How Do You Solve a Problem Like Maria?* can testify, the "tomboy" aspect of Maria's character—and her sense of humor—was terribly important to Lloyd Webber. Having read the lyrics to the show carefully—something that not all producers do—he continually pointed out that in their very first lyric, the nuns complain that Maria "climbs a tree and scrapes her knee." David Ian said that "the only preconception, driven by Andrew, is that historically she has been played by actresses too old for the part." Indeed, both Mary Martin and Petula Clark, though spectacularly successful in their performances, were middle-aged (and Julie Andrews was just shy of thirty). In the end, the lucky winner of the *How Do You Solve a Problem Like Maria?* competition was not only gamine and funny—she was exactly half the age of Mary Martin at the time of the original Broadway production.

There is definitely something Cinderella-like in the story of *The Sound of Music*, and the glass slipper of West End success was a perfect fit for twenty-three-year-old Connie Fisher. Raised in Wales, Fisher moved to London at the age of nineteen, on a full scholarship to Mountview drama school, which concentrates on musical theater. She graduated in 2005 and auditioned and auditioned for every West End job that came her way—always the bridesmaid, but never Cosette, or Truly Scrumptious, or the Woman in

PAGE 178: Overwhelmed by being governess to seven children? Or by a television reality competition? Either way, Connie Fisher demonstrates the confidence that won her both jobs.

LEFT: Zoe Tyler and David Ian, two of the three judges for How Do You Solve a Problem Like Maria? *grill a potential governess. (John Barrowman was the third judge.)*

White. Fisher worked at a Pizza Express and sold advertising over the phone to make ends meet—her only professional stage work was in a Christmas pantomime in the provinces. Still, in the *Maria* competition, she won over millions of viewers and, most important, Lloyd Webber himself. Lloyd Webber's insistence on a youthful Maria had won out—and brought with it one unintended irony; this *Sound of Music* is surely the first major production where the actress playing Liesl (Sophie Bould) would also be the understudy for the actress playing Maria.

For Fisher, the victory was clearly the thrill of a lifetime. She had played Julie Jordan in Rodgers and Hammerstein's *Carousel* in school: "To have done that role has given me an insight into Rodgers and Hammerstein and how much you've got to play with—there is so much to discover in their text," she said, but "Maria . . . was my favorite role of all time. . . and I grabbed it with both hands." The television competition apparently conferred its blessing even on the runners-up; within weeks of the finale, the last five contestants were either employed on the musical stage throughout the UK or had deals pending. "The bottom line is that these girls will have eight weeks of prime-time television [exposure] and will be seen by more people than by a whole career onstage," said Lloyd Webber.

While all eyes were focused on the conclusion of the BBC1 program, plans for the actual stage production were nearly finished. David Ian and Lloyd Webber had chosen as their director Jeremy Sams, a theatrical Renaissance man who had shown his talents as a director, translator, composer, and lyricist. Sams had been working with set and costume designer Robert Jones to create a visual tension on stage that would mirror the emotional conflict of the musical. As Sams told Kate Kellaway of the *Observer*: "[Maria is] a free spirit, a person who changes people by being different herself. The convent was too straitlaced—too perpendicular—for her. She belongs more to mountains, which are curved." Choreographer Arlene Phillips, acclaimed for her work on *Saturday Night Fever* and renowned as a judge on *Strictly Come Dancing*, revealed another side to her modern style by putting the cast through the more legato Austrian folk patterns suggested by Rodgers' music. At the same time, small but incisive edits were made to the score. While honoring the strength of the original material, Lloyd Webber said, "We have added 'I Have Confidence' from the film and substituted 'An Ordinary Couple' with the wonderful 'Something Good' that Richard Rodgers wrote for the movie . . . I believe it is one of his greatest tunes and a fitting swan song from one of the finest melodists of all time."

For all the careful and clever planning prior to opening, the production still tripped and fell over a few stones in its way. Simon Shepherd, a BBC television star who was cast as Captain von Trapp, withdrew after two previews and was swiftly replaced by classical actor Alexander Hanson, who went onstage after only three days of rehearsals. This abrupt shift meant that, over the course of a few days, Fisher had to play opposite three different Captains; Shepherd, the understudy, and Hanson. Fisher's task was made even more difficult by the British child labor law that insisted on there being three separate sets of von Trapp children who must perform in a revolving rotation; simply learning the names of nearly two dozen children would have tried the patience of a seasoned professional.

By the time the show had its opening night on November 15 (the premiere was moved a day later, so as not to compete with another British icon: the opening of the latest James Bond movie), the tills were vibrantly alive; prior to opening, the box office had taken in over £13 million in advance sales. However, the main question at the London Palladium was whether or not Connie Fisher could pull it off. When the curtain fell, it was clear that 2,283 audience members had joined the ranks of the seven von Trapp children and their father; they had fallen in love with Maria. Connie Fisher even won the hearts of the highly skeptical British press. "She is the first real Maria I've seen," wrote Nicholas de Jongh of the *Evening Standard*. "[Fisher] effortlessly transcends the marketing gimmick to deliver a performance that isn't just that of a well-meaning amateur...but comes from an expertly honed and self-assured professional," wrote critic Mark Shenton of the *Sunday Express*. Lloyd Webber, who had more invested in Fisher's success than anyone (other than herself), was elated: "I've never seen a response from the audience like it in my career—maybe the only thing I can compare it with is the first night of *Evita* with Elaine Paige."

If the production at the Palladium won the respect of the critics, so did the redoubtable show itself. It had taken nearly a half-century, but *The Sound of Music* had finally earned good reviews from the British press; in fact, they were the best reviews the musical has ever received—

ABOVE: Designer Robert Jones created c villa for the von Trapps
that shows the sterility and rigidity of their home until Maria arrives;
Sophie Bould (far right) would be the only Liesl to understudy
a Maria in a professional production.

many of them were even downright perceptive. The *Guardian*'s Michael Billington praised the musical as a "melodically abundant show that lauds charity, the act of communal music-making and resistance to political tyranny." Benedict Nightingale in the *Times* wrote: "I acknowledge the pull of a show whose tale draws heavily on three elemental fairy stories: *Cinderella*, *Snow White*, and *Beauty and the Beast*."

Fifty years on, *The Sound of Music* has so penetrated popular culture that is has become an elemental fairy story of its own. In Japan, an anime television series features the adventures of the von Trapp family. In Salzburg, the Salzburg Marionette Theater, which has been performing shortened versions of Mozart's operas for nearly a century, is adding a new title to its repertoire: *The Sound of Music*. This will be the first nonclassical piece by the ensemble that influenced director Robert Wise's vision of "The Lonely Goatherd" for the 1965 movie, and the Marionette Theater will commence a world tour of their adaptation in the winter of 2007.

"The Lonely Goatherd" itself provided an unlikely inspiration for the extravagant pop idol Gwen Stefani. Stefani, the former frontwoman for the ska band No Doubt, has made a huge worldwide name for herself as a singer/trendsetter since going solo in 2004, but she's just a von Trapp fanatic at heart: "I'm like a Trekkie, but for *The Sound of Music*," she told *Entertainment Weekly*. "The first time I ever went on stage, at a high school talent show, the dress that I wore was the dress that Maria wears when she sings 'I Have Confidence.' The drop-waist tweed dress. I had that dress. I made it." Her confidence extends to sampling sections of "The Lonely Goatherd" for her 2006 single, "Wind It Up," which appeared on her album *The Sweet Escape*. (In the video of the single, she can be seen in a nun's habit, dancing in front of a facsimile of the Mirabell Gardens, and sewing costumes out of curtains for her backup dancers.) "Wind It Up" was so successful that it propelled Rodgers and Hammerstein (credited as cowriters for their generous samples of yodel) to their first Top Ten slot on *Billboard*'s Hot 100 charts—an honor they were never able to achieve as a team since they began their partnership in 1943.

If imitation (or sampling) is the sincerest form of flattery, parody must be the sincerest form of immortality. Back in 1966, *MAD*, America's foremost satirical comic magazine, became the first publication to parody *The Sound of Music* with its version of "The Sound of Money," in which the "von Tripes" seem particularly astute about how to wring both tears and dollar bills from the movie audience. As one song parody goes, unhappy kids finally having a good time is what people want: "It will bring us/Back much/DOUGH . . . DOUGH . . . DOUGH . . . DOUGH!" Forty years later, the magazine's TV analogue, *MAD TV* spoofed not only the movie (the variety show is produced by Fox, so the re-creations were particularly accurate), but the DVD extras, for goodness sake. A faux Julie Andrews introduced three "alternate endings" to the movie; in the final one, the von Trapp children manage to elude their Nazi pursuers by using their super powers: eye beams, teleportation, etc. "Gretl—turn to *metal*!" cries Maria in one unforgettable line and, yes, the little girl morphs into Terminator-like titanium invincibility.

The von Trapp family as a superhero team? Well, why not? They have survived just about everything else. *The Sound of Music* seems capable of wringing every possible resonant note out of popular culture. And when you know the notes to wring—you can wring most anything.

ABOVE: *Finding their dream: the finale of the Really Useful Group production of* The Sound of Music. *Alexander Hanson, a last-minute replacement for Captain von Trapp, joins Connie Fisher and Lesley Garrett (below) as the Mother Abbess.*

LEFT: The Sound of Music *broke box office records when it returned to London's West End in late 2006, where the "House Full" sign soon became a familiar sight.*

FAR LEFT: *A sketch for the Salzburg Marionette Theatre's version of the musical.*

CREDITS

FURTHER READING

Anderson, William, *The World of the Trapp Family,* Anderson
Publications, Davison, Michigan, 1998.

Brook-Shepherd, Gordon, *The Anschluss,* J.P. Lippincott Co.
Philadelphia and New York, 1963.

Fordin, Hugh, *Getting to Know Him: A Biography of Oscar
Hammerstein II,* Random House, New York, 1977.

Hirsch, Julia Antopol, *The Sound of Music: The Making of
America's Favorite Movie,* Contemporary Books, Chicago, 1993.

Mander, Raymond and Mitchenson, Joe, *Musical Comedy,*
Taplinger Publishing Co. New York, 1969.

Mordden, Ethan, *Rodgers and Hammerstein,* Abradale Press, New
York, 1992.

"My Favorite Things," Director: Michael Kantor, *Rodgers and
Hammerstein's The Sound of Music: 40th Anniversary Edition,*
20th Century Fox, 2005.

Rodgers, Richard, *Musical Stages, An Autobiography,* Random
House, New York: 1975.

Skinner, Cornelia Otis, *Life With Lindsay and Crouse,* Houghton
Mifflin, Boston, 1976.

The Sound of Music Original Cast Album, Sony Music,
60583, 1998.

The Sound of Music Original London Cast, Angel Records,
52656, 2005.

The Sound of Music Vienna Volksoper Cast, HitSquad, 2005.

Trapp, Maria Augusta, *The Story of the Trapp Family Singers,* J.P.
Lippincott Co. Philadelphia and New York, 1948.

Von Trapp, Maria, *Maria,* Creation Books, New York, 1972.

Von Trapp Family: Harmony and Discord, A&E Home Video, 2000.

Wilk, Max, *Overture and Finale,* Back Stage Books,
New York, 1999.

Your Sound of Music Keepsake, Colorama Verlag, Salzburg, 1993.

Here are some websites for further enjoyment of *The Sound of
Music* saga:

www.bbc.co.uk/maria
The official website of the BBC series "How Do You Solve a
Problem Like Maria?"

www.soundofmusiclondon.com
Official website of the London Palladium production

www.salzburg.sound-of-music.com
Website covering *The Sound of Music* and the city of Salzburg

www.rnh.com
Official website of the Rodgers and Hammerstein Organization

www.josef-weinberger.com
Website for UK and European licensing agents of Rodgers and
Hammerstein, and many others

www.trappfamily.com
The Trapp Family Lodge in Stowe, Vermont, US

www2.salzburg.info
The English-language site for the Salzburg Tourism Office

www.singalonga.net
Website for the *Sing-a-long Sound of Music*

INDEX

First, I would like to extend my profound thanks to Ted Chapin and Bert Fink of the Rodgers and Hammerstein Organization. Their faith in me and their commitment to this project has been exemplary, especially considering the death-defying deadlines under which we all worked. Carol Cornicelli, Kara Darling, and Cindy Boyle, also of R&H, gave me their time, diligence, and consideration.

Michael Kantor of Ghost Light Films has been a great collaborator on several past projects; I thank him for bringing me into the circle of the 40th Anniversary DVD extras he created so skillfully and for assisting with the illustrations to this book. Thanks to Sally Rosenthal as well. And Cornelia Calder dived in headfirst with class and aplomb to coordinate pictures across two continents.

Kate Oldfield and Kate Burkhalter from Pavilion Books were always responsive and supportive to the thousand-and-one details on this book. Kate O, I have met; someday, I hope to meet the other Kate—although her phone manner is impeccable.

My great friend at the Library of Congress, Mark Eden Horowitz, guided me effortlessly through the Oscar Hammerstein holdings there. At the New York Public Library Theatre Collection, Barbara Knowles, Jeremy Megraw, Louise Martzinek, and Tom Lisanti in Reproductions were graceful and resourceful in solving many frantic requests.

Also, Ron Mandelbaum at Photofest went beyond the call of duty and his interest in the project was a great inspiration to me.

Johannes von Trapp, Stefan Herzl, and Rudolf Berger were instrumental in pulling together many of the elements required for the Austrian part of the equation.

Anna Crouse and Fritz Brun gave me many helpful insights on the manuscript, and my eagle-eyed friend and colleague Karyn Gerhard gave the manuscript the most insightful read of all.

In *The Sound of Music*, Captain von Trapp returns from his honeymoon to discover that the Third Reich has offered him a submarine command. When I came home from my honeymoon, I had to face only a volume of page proofs for this book. However, all husbands—whatever the task at hand—need the support and inspiration of great wives to guide them through difficult waters. Georg von Trapp had Maria; I have Genevieve Elam. It seems a very good place to start. LM

Fireside
A Division of Simon & Schuster, Inc.
1230 Avenue of the Americas
New York, NY 10020

Originally published in Great Britain in 2006 by
Pavilion Books, an imprint of Anova Books Company Ltd
Published by arrangement with Anova Books Company Ltd

First Fireside hardcover edition November 2007.

FIRESIDE and colophon are registered trademarks of Simon & Schuster, Inc.

For information about special discounts for bulk purchases, please contact Simon & Schuster Special Sales at 1-800-456-6798 or business@simonandschuster.com.

Designed by Louise Leffler at Sticks Design
10 9 8 7 6 5 4 3 2 1

ISBN-13: 978-1-4165-4954-3
ISBN-10:   1-4165-4954-4

Reproduction by Anorax Imaging Ltd, England
Printed and bound by SNP Leefung, China